NUNAVUT

AN ANNOTATED BIBLIOGRAPHY

Elaine L. Simpson
Linda N. Seale
Robin Minion

Cataloguing-in-Publication Data

Simpson, Elaine L.
    Nunavut: an annotated bibliography / Elaine L.
    Simpson, Linda N. Seale, Robin Minion.
    Edmonton, Alta.: Canadian Circumpolar Institute
    and the University of Alberta Library, 1994.
    (Northern reference series, no. 4)

    ISBN 0-919058-90-6

    1. Inuit --Northwest Territories --Legal Status,
       laws, etc. -- Bibliography. 2. Nunavut (N.W.T.) --
       Bibliography. I. Seale, Linda N. II. Minion,
       Robin. III. Canadian Circumpolar Institute
       IV. University of Alberta Library. V. Title.

    Z 1392 N
    FC 4173.3

CONTENTS

INTRODUCTION

The compilation of this selected annotated bibliography on the literature of Nunavut was prompted by several events. The approval of the boundary for Nunavut in May 1992 and the official signing of the **Nunavut Land Claim Agreement** in 1993, have made Nunavut a reality in the political, social and economic landscape of Canada. The passage of the **Nunavut Act 1993** marked both the successful conclusion of almost thirty years of work by the Inuit on the landclaim, and the start of work on implementation for the target date of 1999.

The Nunavut Bibliography is aimed at those individuals who require an understanding of the background concepts and current issues relating to Nunavut in order to work productively in this environment. Secondarily, the bibliography will be of use to students, the general public and researchers whose primary area of interest may not be landclaims. The bibliography covers the historical development of the political concept of Nunavut to December 1993. It includes key works on related developments in other Canadian aboriginal landclaims, as well as on topics of current importance, such as land use management and devolution of powers as reflected in the articles of the **Nunavut Land Claim Agreement**. It is a companion piece to the **Nunavut Atlas**[1].

The literature referenced in this bibliography includes both published documents and "grey" literature. Examples of the types of documents referenced are records of court cases, legislation, reports of Royal Commissions and other government publications, as well as position papers and proposals from native and government organizations. Journal literature, conference proceedings, theses and chapters and papers from monographs are also included. Newspaper articles have been excluded as too numerous and repetitive.

Material for the bibliography was located through searches of the catalogues of several major northern collections: Canadian Circumpolar Library, Arctic Institute of North America, the Canada Department of Indian Affairs Northern Departmental Library and the Government of the Northwest Territories Legislative Library. Other library searches included the University of Alberta Library on-line catalogue and the Alberta Legislature Library on-line catalogue. Selected on-line databases were searched in DIALOG. CD-ROM searches included Arctic and Antarctic Regions, PolarPac, Microlog and Canadian Business and Current Affairs. Printed indexes searched include: Index to Canadian Legal Literature, Canadian Government Publications Catalogue, the Canadian Periodical Index and Boreal Northern Titles (KWIC) Index.

---

[1] Rick Riewe, <u>Nunavut Atlas</u>, (Edmonton: Canadian Circumpolar Institute and the Tungavik Federation of Nunavut, 1992).

Documents not held by the Canadian Circumpolar Library or the University of Alberta Library were lent or supplied by Canada Department of Indian Affairs Northern Departmental Library, Government of the Northwest Territories Legislative Library, the Tungavik Federation of Nunavut and Dr. R. Riewe, of the Canadian Circumpolar Institute. The majority of the annotations were written by the compilers of the bibliography.

Acknowledgments

This bibliography was produced with financial assistance from the Canadian Circumpolar Institute, as part of its "Northern Reference Series". The compilers gratefully acknowledge the professional assistance of: Dr. Cliff Hickey and Dr. Rick Riewe (Canadian Circumpolar Institute); Ernie Ingles, Margo Young, Barbara Burrows, Gene Olson, Pat Rempel and Caron Rollins (University of Alberta Library); the Tungavik Federation of Nunavut and Vera Raschke (Government of the Northwest Territories Legislative Library).

Organization

This section explains the general arrangement of the bibliography, gives advice to users, and provides some specific information relevant to the chronological list. The purpose of the chronology has been to record the major events (since 1867) that have contributed to the concept of a Nunavut territory and the official signing of the Nunavut Land Claim Agreement in 1993. No attempt has been made to give due weight to the relative significance of each event listed in the chronology.

Several acronyms occur in titles cited in the bibliography. An alphabetical list of these acronyms has been provided because of their limited currency and frequently specialized use.

The author index is arranged alphabetically by author's last name. The title index is arranged alphabetically by the title of the publication or the title of the article. The numbers in the indexes are the citation numbers which appear next to each citation included in the bibliography. The indexed items may have more than one citation number as they may have been included in more than one section of the bibliography.

The majority of citations included in this bibliography on the development of Nunavut are held in the Canadian Circumpolar Library, at the University of Alberta. The names and addresses of other libraries having materials relating to the development of Nunavut have been included.

The actual bibliography is organized into seven sections:

- Section 1 includes general works and overviews of the topic

- Section 2 deals with the roots of the idea to 1963 when division of the Northwest Territories was first discussed by the Federal Government

- Section 3 covers the period 1964-1982, the years when the concept was developed, modified and approved in principle

- Section 4 (1983-1993) deals with the resolution of problems and construction of the Agreement

- Section 5 lists works on other landclaims within Canada for comparative purposes

- Section 6 provides selected references on landclaim settlements elsewhere, such as Alaska, Greenland and Australia

- Section 7 covers a number of miscellaneous topics relevant to the development of Nunavut.

CANADIAN LIBRARY LOCATIONS

ARCTIC INSTITUTE OF NORTH AMERICA
The University of Calgary
2500 University Drive N.W.
Calgary Alberta T2N 1N4
Phone: (403) 220-7515
Fax: (403) 282-4609

**CANADA. DEPARTMENT OF INDIAN AFFAIRS NORTHERN
        DEVELOPMENTAL LIBRARY**
Ottawa , Ontario K1A 0H4
Phone: (819) 997-0811
Fax: 997-0511/4/8

CANADIAN CIRCUMPOLAR LIBRARY
Cameron
The University of Alberta
Edmonton, Alberta T6G 2J8
Phone: (403) 492-4409
Fax: (403) 492-2721

LEGISLATIVE LIBRARY
Government of the Northwest Territories
P.O. Box 1320
Yellowknife, N.W.T. X1A 2L9
Phone: (403) 669-2202
Fax: (403) 873-0207

ACRONYMS

AIGP	Arctic Islands Game Preserve
ANCSA	Alaska Native Claims Settlement Act
BRIA	Baffin Region Inuit Association
CA	Constitutional Alliance
CARC	Canadian Arctic Resources Committee
CEC	Community Enrollment Committee
CLINT	Community Land Identification Negotiation Team
COPE	Committee for Original Peoples' Entitlement
CYI	Council of Yukon Indians
DIAND	Department of Indian Affairs and Northern Development
DIOS	Designated Inuit Organizations
EARP	Environmental Assessment Review Process
EAS	Eastern Arctic Study
ESRF	Environmental Studies Revolving Fund
FEARO	Federal Environmental Assessment Review Process
GNWT	Government of the Northwest Territories
ICNI	Inuit Committee on National Issues
IIBA's	Inuit Impact and Benefit Agreements
ITC	Inuit Tapirisat of Canada
JBNQA	James Bay and Northern Quebec Agreement

KIA	Keewatin Lands Authority
LIP	Land Identification Project
MOU	Memorandum of Understanding
NAPO	Nunavut Affairs Planning Office
NCF	Nunavut Constitutional Forum
NEQA	Northeastern Quebec Agreement
NGB	Nunavut Governing Body
NIRB	Nunavut Impact Review Board
NLA	Nunavut Lands Authority
NWMB	Nunavut Wildlife Management Board
NWT	Northwest Territories
N.W.T.	Northwest Territories
SEARP	Socio-Economic Environmental Assessment Review Panel
TFN	Tungavik Federation of Nunavut
WAIP	Wildlife Agreement-in-Principle
WCF	Western Constitutional Forum
YANSI	Yukon Association for Non-Status Indians
YNB	Yukon Native Brotherhood

THE DEVELOPMENT OF NUNAVUT: A CHRONOLOGY

1867	The Constitution Act assigned to Parliament the responsibility for Indians.
1868	Rupert's Land and North Western Territory ceded by the Hudson's Bay Company to the Crown, and admitted to Canadian Union by British-Order-In-Council, confirming aboriginal land rights. [Rupert's Land Act, 1868 (U.K.), 31 & 32 Vic. c. 105]. The Manitoba Act was passed establishing the province of Manitoba.
1870	Northwest territories created. [Temporary Government of Rupert's Land Act 1869, 1870 (Can.), 32 & 33 Vic. c.3]. The Manitoba Act was passed establishing the province of Manitoba.
1875	The Northwest Territories Act was passed, providing the basis for present constitutional and legislative status for the Northwest Territories, with a fully elected assembly resulting in 1881.
1876	The first Indian Act imposed a uniform system of band government subject to federal control and consolidated all previous legislation concerning Indians. The District of Keewatin was established.
1877	The District of Keewatin was reduced through the outward extension of Manitoba's boundary.
1880	The Arctic Islands were transferred to Canada from Great Britain. The Department of Indian Affairs was established.

1896	The first Act for the preservation of game in the Northwest Territories was put into force.
1898	Yukon was established as a separate territory by the Yukon Territory Act.
1899	Treaty 8 was signed, affecting some areas of the present Northwest Territories.
1905	Two acts, "The Alberta Act" and "The Saskatchewan Act" were given Royal assent on July 20; and on September 1, 1905 establishing the provinces of Alberta and Saskatchewan. [Alberta Act, 1905 (Can.), 4-5 Ed.. VII c.3]. [Saskatchewan Act, 1905 (Can.), 4-5 Ed. VII c.42]. An amendment to the Northwest Territories Act provided for the appointment of a Commissioner and a Council of not more than four to assist him to oversee the remainder of the Northwest Territories. It also provided for the transfer of the seat of government to Ottawa.
1912	The boundaries of Manitoba, Ontario and Quebec were again extended northward The Nishga Indians of British Columbia initiated the first legally-constituted landclaim action against the federal government.
1921	The Northwest Territories Council was enlarged to six members. Treaty 11 was signed with the Dene of the Mackenzie Valley.
1922	The Indian Act was changed to include the administration of the Inuit (Eskimo). [14-15 Geo. V. ch. 47]
1926	By Order in Council the "Arctic Islands Game Preserve (AIGP) was established encompassing the High Arctic Islands, northwestern Baffin Island and islands west to and including northeastern Banks Island and a small portion of the mainland to bolster Canada's claims to sovereignty.

1929	The boundaries of the Arctic Islands Game Preserve (AIGP) were expanded.
1942	The boundaries of the Arctic Islands Game Preserve (AIGP) were expanded to encompass all of the Eastern Arctic with the exception of the southern Keewatin and some islands in Hudson Bay.
1951	The Northwest Territories Act was amended allowing for the first election of members to the Northwest Territories Council. The Council was enlarged to eight, three members had to be elected from constituencies in the District of Mackenzie and a least one yearly session of the Council had to be held in the Northwest Territories. A new Indian Act (1951 (Can.), 15 Geo. VI c. 29) was passed, protecting Indian lands from alienation, and Indian property from depredation, as well as providing for a form of local government and for the eventual end of Indian status.
1953-1954	As a result of concern regarding Arctic sovereignty and Cold War politics, the federal government reorganized northern administration. Northern Service Officers were sent from Ottawa to the Northwest Territories to establish settlements and local government. Inuit education and health were to be the responsibility of the federal government.
1959	The "Nelson Commission" was appointed to investigate the unfulfilled provisions of Treaty 8 and Treaty 11.
1960	Aboriginal people in the Northwest Territories were accorded the right to vote in federal elections. The new administration region of Mackenzie was created with administration from Fort Smith.
1961	The first exploratory oil-well in the Canadian High Arctic was drilled on Melville Island.

1962	On September 27; the Conservative government in its Throne Speech indicated that measures would be introduced to provide greater self-government leading to the creation of new provinces in Canada's North.
1963	On May 21; the Liberal government introduced legislation (which was never implemented) proposing the division of the Northwest Territories into the Mackenzie and Nunassiaq Territories. A full time Commissioner for the Northwest Territories was appointed.
1965	Dean A.W.R. Carrothers was appointed by the federal government to head an "Advisory Commission on the Development of Government of the Northwest Territories" (Carrothers Commission).
1966	The Carrothers Commission advised against division of the Northwest Territories for the next ten years, but two federal constituencies were created. The Territorial Council abolished the Arctic Islands Game Preserve (AIGP) and brought the area within the same legislative framework as the rest of the Northwest Territories.
1967	The Northwest Territories Council moved from Ottawa to Yellowknife.
1969	Nishga Indians of British Columbia went to court for a declaration that their title had never been surrendered by treaty or otherwise extinguished. "Statement of the Government of Canada on Indian Policy" (White Paper) was published, recommending repeal of the Indian Act and abolition of all legal distinctions between natives and non-natives. In December; Dr. Lloyd Barber was appointed as Indian Claims Commissioner to receive and study Indian grievances and claims, and recommend measures to be taken by the government to resolve them.

1970	The Committee For Original Peoples' Entitlement (COPE) was formally incorporated on September 25; which marked a turning point for northern natives, in giving them a recognized voice from which to express their concerns over aboriginal rights.

The Indian Brotherhood of the Northwest Territories was established to deal with concerns over terms of Treaty 8 (1899-1900) and Treaty 11 (1921-1922). |
| **1971** | The Inuit Tapirisat of Canada (ITC) was established to speak with a united voice on issues concerning development of the Canadian North and preservation of Inuit culture. |
| **1972** | The Metis and Non-Status Native Association of the NWT was incorporated. (The name later changed to Metis Association of the N.W.T. and then to Metis Nation, N.W.T.).

At the Inuit Tapirisat of Canada Conference, land claims were confirmed as the highest priority. |
| **1973** | The Paulette Caveat (a declaration of prior interest in the land) to 450,000 square miles of traditional land was filed in the Supreme Court of the N.W.T. by the Dene, illustrating their aboriginal title. It was later overturned by the Supreme Court of Canada on technical grounds. (Re Paulette's Application ... (1973) 6 W.W.R. 97 (NWT S.C.)

Calder v. Attorney-General of B.C. decided by the Supreme Court of Canada, and later the federal government reversed its position that aboriginal title was not a concept existing in Canadian common law. (Calder et al. v. Attorney General of British Columbia, (1973) S.C.R. 313)

The Yukon Native Indian Brotherhood presented a land claim proposal for status and non-status Indians in the Yukon (Together Today for Our Children Tomorrow). The federal government agreed to negotiate, implying some recognition of rights.

The Canadian government announced that it would establish an Office of Native Claims to negotiate "comprehensive claims," claims for land not covered by treaty, and "specific claims," claims based on treaties, the Indian Act, or other legislation. |

1973	The James Bay Hydro-Electric Project, announced by Quebec Premier Robert Bourassa in 1971, was contested by the Cree with the Quebec Superior Court issuing an interim injunction halting the project.
1974	The Office of Native Claims was established within the Department of Indian and Northern Affairs to evaluate and negotiate Indian land claims.
	Milton Freeman's "Inuit Land Use and Occupancy Project" conducted in 1974, defined boundaries on Inuit land use in Kitmeot, Keewatin, and Baffin. (In 1979 these boundaries were adopted as Nunavut boundaries.)
	The Indians and Inuit of northern Quebec signed an agreement-in-principle with the Quebec and Canadian governments to settle their land claims in northern Quebec.
1975	The first fully-elected Northwest Territories Assembly, was held signifying the end of political appointments.
	Mr. Justice Thomas Berger opened the Mackenzie Valley Pipeline Inquiry to examine the terms and conditions on constructing a pipeline in the Mackenzie Valley.
	The Dene Declaration was unanimously passed by a Joint General Assembly (of the Indian Association) in Fort Simpson, proposing self-government for the Dene, although the federal government did not view political issues as negotiable.
	The James Bay and Northern Quebec Agreement was signed between the Grand Council of the Crees (Quebec), Northern Quebec Inuit Association and the Government of Quebec, the James Bay Energy Corporation, the James Bay Development Corporation, the Quebec Hydro-electric Commission (Hydro-Quebec) and the Government of Canada. It was the first major agreement between the crown and native peoples in Canada.
	On Oct. 9; the Commission on Home Rule for Greenland was established.
1976	On Feb. 27; the Inuit Tapirisat of Canada (ITC) proposed division of the Northwest Territories, (as part of the Inuit land claim), and the creation of a new territory in the eastern Arctic to be called Nunavut (Our Land). The Nunavut Proposal included the Inuvialuit region (represented by COPE).

1976	The Inuvialuit split off to settle their land claim independently of the Inuit Tapirisat of Canada.
	The Special Electoral Boundaries Commission recommended division of the N.W.T. into two electoral districts: Nunatsiaq and the Western Arctic.
	The Dene of the Northwest Territories presented a draft agreement-in-principle to the government of Canada which proposed an Indian government for the Northwest Territories with powers like that of a province. The Metis of the Northwest Territories did not support this proposal and asked for separate funds to fund their own claim research.
1977	The Metis Association of the NWT submitted a claim paper "Our Land, Our Culture, Our Future", to the federal government proposing that the N.W.T. be divided by extending the Manitoba/Saskatchewan boundary northwards.
	The Committee for Original Peoples' Entitlement (COPE) presented "Inuvialuit Nunangat" a proposal for an agreement-in-principle to achieve the settlement of Inuvialuit land rights in the Western Arctic region of the Northwest Territories and the Yukon.
	C. M. Drury was appointed by the federal government to conduct an inquiry on constitutional development in the Northwest Territories.
	The Berger Report on the Mackenzie Valley Pipeline Inquiry was published recommending the postponement of the pipeline for ten years.
	On December 14; the NWT Inuit Land Claims Commission put forward a proposal to the federal government calling for the formation of a new territory and government along the lines of Inuit political institutions. (Proposed Agreement-in-Principle for the Establishment of Inuit Rights Between the Inuit of Nunavut and the Government of Canada.)
1978	A federal land claims proposal entitled "Dene and Metis Claims in the Mackenzie Valley", was rejected by both the Dene and Metis, resulting in the withdrawal of federal funding for negotiations until a single claim could be produced for both groups.
	The name "National Indian Brotherhood of the NWT" was formally changed to "Dene Nation" at the Dene National Assembly.

1978	On October 31, the Committee for Original Peoples' Entitlement (COPE) signed the "Inuvialuit Land Rights Settlement Agreement-in-Principle" with the Canadian government to settle the Inuvialuit (Inuit of the western arctic) land claim in the western arctic.

The Home Rule Act for Greenland was adopted by the Danish Parliament on November 17 (Conf. Act no. 577, November 29, 1978, Lovtidende, A, 1978, p. 1879). |
| **1979** | On January 17; the population of Greenland approved by referendum the entering into force of the Home Rule Act in Greenland on May 1, 1979.

The Metis Association announced that the Dene Nation would be responsible for negotiating aboriginal rights for both the Dene and the Metis.

The Northwest territories was divided into two electoral districts for a federal election: Nunatsiaq and the Western Arctic.

On May 1, 1979 Greenland achieved home rule as a Danish province resulting in a unique situation of a native state within the Danish Kingdom.

In September; the Inuit Tapirisat of Canada (ITC) at its Annual General Assembly in Igloolik, released a discussion paper entitled "Political Development in Nunavut" which called for the division of the Northwest Territories within ten years and provincehood for a Nunavut Territory within an additional five years.

The Inuit of Baker Lake, N.W.T., took the federal government to court to protect their land from mining operations and to clarify the issue of aboriginal rights. On November 15, 1979 Mr. Justice Patrick Mahoney ruled that the Baker Lake area was subject to the aboriginal rights of the Inuit living there. The Baker Lake Case established aboriginal rights in the Canadian legal system for the first time.

A new Legislative Assembly of the N.W.T. was elected, resulting in an Assembly where native people were a majority.

On November 16; the Legislative Assembly created the Special Committee on Unity. |

1980	In January; the "Drury Report" (Report of the Special Representative on Constitutional Development in the Northwest Territories), recommended that the N.W.T. should remain a single political unit and should not be divided, and that residents should assume the major responsibility for determining the direction and pace of political change in the N.W.T.
	Funding was reinstated to develop a land settlement position for Dene and Metis of the Mackenzie Valley.
	In October; at its Annual General Meeting, the Inuit Tapirisat of Canada (ITC) passed a resolution calling for the creation of Nunavut.
	On October 22; the Report of The Special Committee on Unity was tabled at the third session of the Northwest Territories Assembly at Frobisher Bay. The report recommended a commitment by the Assembly to divide the Northwest Territories subject to the will of the people to be determined by a plebiscite and to request the federal government to divide the Northwest Territories if the plebiscite is answered affirmatively.
	During its November 1980 session at Frobisher Bay, the Legislative Assembly of the Northwest Territories voted in support of a division of the territories.
	In November; "The Special Committee on the Impact of Division " was established by the Legislative Assembly to prepare an objective study of the impact of division of the Northwest Territories as a whole and upon its several parts and their people.
1981	In May; the Legislative Assembly voted in favor of plebiscite concerning the creation of Nunavut.
	In November; the Legislative Assembly adopted a plebiscite ordinance and set the date, April 14, 1982 and the question "Do you think the Northwest Territories should be divided?" Yes or no.
	The Dene Nation and Metis Association proposed the establishment of a province-like jurisdiction called Denendeh in their discussion paper "Public Government For the People of the North".
	In December the federal government restated its 1973 policy on comprehensive claims in a paper titled "In All Fairness".

1982	In February; several members of the Legislative Assembly, the Inuit Tapirisat of Canada, the Dene Nation, the Metis Association of the NWT and the Committee For Original Peoples' Entitlement united to form the Constitutional Alliance (CA).
	On April 14; a plebiscite was held on the question of division of the Northwest Territories into Denendeh and Nunavut, which was supported by the people of the Northwest Territories.
	The Constitution Act 1982 was enacted elaborating aboriginal and treaty rights.
	In May; the Legislative Assembly passed a motion recommending that the federal government appoint a federal boundaries commission.
	The federal government released "Outstanding Business" which clarified its policy on specific claims. The statement expressed the government's aim to meet its legal obligations as set out in post-confederation treaties and the Indian Act.
	The boundaries commission was not appointed, and the Constitutional Alliance (CA) broke itself into two sub committees, the Western Constitutional Forum (WCF) and the Nunavut Constitutional Forum (NCF) to pursue the matter of division of the Northwest Territories and constitutional development.
	The Tungavik Federation of Nunavut (TFN) was established to negotiate land claims as a political arm of the Inuit Tapirisat of Canada (ITC).
1983	The Nunavut Constitutional Form (NCF) published "Nunavut" and "Building Nunavut".
	The "Report of the Special Committee on Indian Self-Government" (the Penner Report) unanimously agreed that the aboriginal right to self-government should be entrenched in the Constitution.
1984	In January the Council of Yukon Indians signed an agreement-in-principle to settle their land claim with the federal government.
	Tungavik Federation of Nunavut (TFN) and the Committee for Original Peoples' Entitlement (COPE) signed a boundary and overlap agreement.

1984	On June 5; the federal government signed the Western Arctic Claim: Inuvialuit Final Agreement with the Committee for Original Peoples' Entitlement (COPE) representing the Inuvialuit of the Western Arctic. This was the first comprehensive landclaims settlement north of the 60th parallel. On October 10; the Western Constitutional Forum (WCF) released a report entitled "Resource Management Boundary Problems" which identified a number of potential overlapping resources and compared five boundary alternatives.
1985	The Minister of Indian and Northern Affairs, David Crombie, announced to the Legislative Assembly that the federal government was willing to support division of the N.W.T. upon finalization of a boundary for division. A federal task force to review comprehensive claims policy issued its report "Living Treaties: Lasting Agreements" (Coolican Report).
1986	The Tungavik Federation of Nunavut (TFN) and the Dene/Metis signed a boundary and overlap agreement that established a boundary through the Kitikmeot and Keewatin regions.
1987	The federal government issued a document entitled "Comprehensive Land Claims Policy", which modified federal policy by allowing federal officials to consider specific options or alternatives in a claims settlement which did not formally extinguish aboriginal title. On January 15; the leaders of the Constitutional Alliance (CA) signed the Iqaluit Agreement which was premised on the still unratified 1986 Tungavik Federation of Nunavut (TFN) and Dene/Metis boundary and overlap agreement. On March 12; the document "Boundary and Constitutional Agreement for the Implementation of Division of the Northwest Territories between the Western Constitutional Forum and the Nunavut Constitutional Forum" was approved by the Legislative Assembly. It was recommended that a plebiscite on the proposed boundary be held.

1987	The Tungavik Federation on Nunavut (TFN) and the Dene/Metis were unable to come to a common understanding of their proposed 1986 boundary and overlap agreement, resulting in the collapse of the Iqaluit Agreement and the cancellation of the upcoming plebiscite.
1988	The Department of Indian Affairs and Northern Development released a document entitled "A Northern Political and Economic Framework", which supported the goals of establishing northern government, settling landclaims and promoting economic development.
	The "Comprehensive Land Claim Agreement-in-Principle Between Canada and the Dene Nation and the Metis Association of the Northwest Territories" was signed.
1990	On March 31; "Comprehensive Land Claim Umbrella Final Agreement Between the Government of Canada, the Council For Yukon Indians and the Government of the Yukon" was initialed.
	In April the Dene/Metis signed their final landclaim agreement with the federal government.
	On April 30; "An Agreement-in-Principle Between the Inuit of the Nunavut Settlement Area and Her Majesty in Right of Canada" was reached.
	In July the Dene and Metis rejected their comprehensive landclaim settlement with the federal government because of concern over the provision that would have them surrender their aboriginal rights. The Gwich'in left to settle their claim on a regional basis.
1991	In July the Gwich'in (Kutchin), Athapaskan Indians of the Mackenzie delta reached a landclaims settlement with the federal government based on the agreement rejected by the Dene and Metis of the Northwest Territories in April, 1990.
	On December 7; the Council of Yukon Indians voted to accept their umbrella final agreement on their landclaim with the federal government.
	Indian Affairs Minister Tom Siddon announced on December 16, that the government had reached a final agreement with the Inuit (Tungavik Federation of Nunavut) of the eastern Arctic.

1991	Former N.W.T. Commissioner John Parker was appointed as an advisor to resolve the landclaims boundary dispute between the Tungavik Federation on Nunavut (TFN) and the Dene/Metis claims. "The Parker Line" was established as the boundary of Nunavut.
	The Royal Commission on Aboriginal Peoples was appointed.
1992	In January the Board of Directors of the Tungavik Federation of Nunavut accepted the Agreement Between the Inuit of the Nunavut Settlement Area and Her Majesty the Queen in Right of Canada, and passed a resolution recommending that the Inuit ratify the agreement.
	On January 31, the wording of the plebiscite question was announced at the Nunavut Leaders' Summit in Iqaluit, N.W.T.
	On February 17; the Government Leader of the Legislative Assembly in a letter to the Chief Plebiscite Officer established May 4, 1992 as the date for a plebiscite on the boundary for division.
	In April the Nunavut Political Accord committed the federal and Northwest Territories governments to negotiate with the Inuit the legislation to create the Nunavut Territory Government.
	The final "Comprehensive Land Claim Agreement Between Her Majesty the Queen in Right of Canada and the Gwich'in as Represented by the Gwich'in Tribal Council" was signed on April 22.
	On May 4 the residents of the Northwest Territories narrowly approved the creation on Nunavut in a plebiscite.
	The Inuit in a vote held on November 3-6, approved the Agreement and authorized it to be signed by the duly appointed officers of the Tungavik Federation of Nunavut.
1993	It was decided that the Tungavik Federation of Nunavut Tungavik Inc. would direct transition to Nunavut and in March a Nunavut wide election was held to elect the executive officers.
	On May 25; in Iqaluit, Northwest Territories, the final Agreement Between the Inuit of the Nunavut Settlement Area and Her Majesty the Queen in Right of Canada was signed.

BIBLIOGRAPHY

SECTION 1: GENERAL/OVERVIEWS

1-1   Aboriginal Self-Government and Constitutional Reform: Setbacks,
        Opportunities, and Arctic Experiences: a National Conference Held in
        Ottawa 9-10 June 1987. (1988). Ottawa, Ont.: Canadian Arctic Resources
        Committee.

        Proceedings of a conference jointly organized by the Canadian Arctic
        Resources Committee and the Inuit Committee on National Issues.

1-2   Asch, M. (1984). Home and Native Land: Aboriginal Rights and the Canadian
        Constitution. Toronto, Ont.: Methuen.

        This book is divided into two major sections. The first focuses on
        definitions and provides a detailed account of the meaning of the phrase
        "aboriginal rights" as used by the government and the aboriginal peoples.
        The second is devoted to the question of political rights and the means by
        which this issue can be resolved.

1-3   Bartlett, R. H. (1991). Resource Development and Aboriginal Land Rights.
        Calgary, Alta.: Canadian Institute of Resources Law.

        These papers examine the relationship between aboriginal title to land and
        the development of natural resources, both in the current and historical
        context, with an emphasis on western Canada. Includes the treaty clauses
        providing for establishment of reserves.

1-4   Bennett, D. (1982). Subsistence v. Commercial Use: the Meaning of These
        Words in Relation to Hunting and Fishing by Canada's Native Peoples.
        Working Paper, 3. Ottawa, Ont.: Canadian Arctic Resources Committee.

        Identifies the use and meaning of the terms domestic, subsistence and
        commercial in the statutes and regulations which apply to native use of fish
        and wildlife in Canada, particularly northern Canada.

1-5   Boldt, M., & Long, J. A. (1985). The Quest for Justice: Aboriginal Peoples and
        Aboriginal Rights. Toronto, Ont.: University of Toronto Press.

        Papers discussing land rights and concerns of the Metis and Inuit. Discusses
        native rights in broader contexts such as historical, legal, constitutional, and
        political areas. Contains twenty-three papers from representatives of various
        aboriginal people's organizations, governments, and academic disciplines.
        Also includes key constitutional documents from 1763. Various
        constitutional questions relating to Canadian natives, such as land rights are
        addressed.

1-6   Bone, R. M. (1992). The Geography of the Canadian North: Issues and
        Challenges. Don Mills, Ont.: Oxford University Press.

        This discussion of the Canadian North (Northwest Territories and Yukon as
        well as northern Quebec and northern parts of the provinces) considers
        perceptions of the north, physical geography, history, economic
        development, landclaims and future prospects.

1-7   Canada. Dept. of Indian and Northern Affairs. Office of Native Claims (1978).
        Native Claims: Policy, Processes and Perspectives: Opinion Paper. Ottawa,
        Ont.: Department of Indian and Northern Affairs.

        Discusses history and current status of native claims in Canada.

1-8   Coates, K. S. (1992). Aboriginal Land Claims in Canada: A Regional
        Perspective. Toronto, Ont.: Copp Clark Pitman.

        This book is designed to be an introduction to native landclaims in Canada,
        to facilitate discussion of aboriginal landclaims, and to provide readers with
        some of the raw data necessary to judge the complexity of the issues for
        themselves. Includes treaty and comprehensive claims.

1-9   Coates, K. S., & Morrison William R. (1989). For Purposes of Dominion:
        Essays in Honour of Morris Zaslow. North York, Ont.: Captus University
        Publications.

        This collection of 16 papers covers the history of the administration of the
        Canadian north, documents changing attitudes to Indian, Metis, Dene and
        Inuit and reviews current issues such as landclaims and pipeline
        construction.

1-10   Cozzetto, D. A. (1990). Governance in Nunavut. Doctoral Thesis. Virginia
        Polytechnic Institute and State University, Virginia.

        Examines a series of political-administrative strategies designed to assist in
        establishing a native form of government in Nunavut, the new Inuit territory
        in the eastern part of the Canadian Arctic. The study explores a number of
        models for post-claims governance which may provide a means to maintain
        the distinctive aspects of aboriginal society, economy and culture, while
        recognizing the need for a continued active native participation in the
        Canadian federation.

1-11   Crowe, K. J. (1990, November). Claims On The Land. Arctic Circle, 1(3), 14-23.

        Summary of the background, character, and process of northern landclaims
        (Yukon, Nunavut, Denendeh, Northern Quebec, and Labrador) including a
        map of settlements to date and table summarizing progress and features of
        agreements, including the Nunavut Agreement in Principle of April 1990.
        (Continued by article by the same author in Arctic Circle 1(4) (January-
        February, 1991), pp. 31-35).

1-12   Crowe, K. J. (1991, January). Claims On the Land. <u>Arctic Circle</u>, 1(4), 31-35.

Analysis of problems in settling landclaims in northern Canada, including James Bay, COPE, Nunavut, and Denendeh, with comparisons with Alaska and Greenland. (Continues article by the same author in Arctic Circle 1(3) (November-December, 1990), pp. 14- 23).

1-13   Cumming, P. A. (1977). <u>Canada: Native Land Rights and Northern Development</u>. IWGIA Document, 26. Copenhagen, Denmark: International Work Group For Indigenous Affairs.

History of native rights and landclaims in Canada. Includes a discussion of the Nunavut proposal made to the Federal Cabinet in 1976.

1-14   Curwin, K. (1990, September). A Federal Report Card. <u>Arctic Circle</u>, 1(2), 14- 21.

Discussion of northern attitudes towards the Meech Lake Accord and the actions of the Federal Government of Canada on landclaims in Nunavut, Denendeh, and Yukon.

1-15   Dacks, G. (1981). <u>A Choice of Futures: Politics in the Canadian North</u>. Agincourt, Ont.: Methuen.

Examines inter-related social and political issues of the Canadian north, including native claims, political development and economic future.

1-16   Dacks, G. (1990). <u>Devolution and Constitutional Development in the Canadian North</u>. Ottawa, Ont.: Carleton University Press.

A collection of papers on the process of devolution in the Yukon and Northwest Territories. Discusses many aspects of constitutional devolution including historical perspectives, effect on forest fire and wildlife management, health care, local government, oil and gas accords, regional development, and politics.

1-17   Dacks, G. (1991). Devolution and Northern Provincehood. In C. Robinson (Editor), <u>Old Pathways and New Directions: Towards a Sustainable Future: Proceedings From the Arctic Institute of North America's First Annual Kluane Lake Conference Held at the Kluane Field Station, the Yukon, in September 1989</u>, (pp. 14-32). Calgary, Alta.: Arctic Institute of North America.

This paper argues that, if constitutional development is to endure and thrive, it must respond to the needs and the special self-definitions of northerners. The politics of Canada in general and the North in particular give the process of the intergovernmental devolution of power an important role in determining the responsiveness and legitimacy of the future governments of northern Canada.

1-18   Dacks, G. (1990). Political and Constitutional Development in the Yukon and the Northwest Territories: the Influence of Devolution. <u>Northern Review</u>, 5, 102-130.

        Examines how devolution of jurisdiction from government of Canada to territorial governments is affecting linked processes of constitutional and political development in northern Canada.

1-19   Dacks, G., & Coates, K. (1988). <u>Northern Communities: the Prospects for Empowerment</u>. Boreal Institute for Northern Studies Occasional Publication, 25. Edmonton, Alta.: Boreal Institute for Northern Studies.

        Papers from a workshop given at the "Knowing the North Conference" which assess the prospects for the greater empowerment of the smaller, primarily aboriginal communities of the North.

1-20   Daniel, R. C. (1980). <u>A History of Native Claims Processes in Canada 1867-1979</u>. Ottawa, Ontario: Research Branch, Dept. of Indian and Northern Affairs.

        An historical background survey of the various processes and mechanisms used by government since Confederation in an attempt to resolve native claims.

1-21   Demers, C. (1986). Perspectives on Native Land-Claims Policy: Background Paper. In <u>National and Regional Interests in the North: Third National Workshop on People, Resources, and the Environment North of 60, Yellowknife, Northwest Territories 1-3 June 1983</u>, Yellowknife, 1983 (pp. 87-106). Ottawa, Ont.: Canadian Arctic Resources Committee.

        Brief history of federal native claims policy and the claims process in Canada, with a summary of the COPE claim (Committee for Original Peoples' Entitlement) and the Nunavut claim by TFN (Tungavik Federation of Nunavut).

1-22   Dickerson, M. O. (1992). <u>Whose North?: Political Change, Political Development, and Self-Government in the Northwest Territories</u>. Vancouver, B.C., Calgary, Alberta: UBC Press and the Arctic Institute of North America.

        The text discusses the development of an innovative governmental process in the Northwest Territories, to deal with issues of Native cultures, landclaims, division and economic development.

1-23   Doering, R. L. (1986). Natural Resource Jurisdiction and Political Development in the North: the Case of Nunavut: Background Paper. In <u>National and Regional Interests in the North: Third National Workshop on People, Resources, and the Environment North of 60, Yellowknife, Northwest Territories 1-3 June 1983,</u> (pp. 117-131). Ottawa, Ont.: Canadian Arctic Resources Committee.

        This paper summarizes the federal and northern positions on political change in the Northwest Territories and the formation of Nunavut. It also considers the issues of resource revenue sharing, native claims, and Nunavut jurisdiction to regulate environmental and socio-economic aspects of resource developments.

1-24   Duffy, R. Q. (1988). The Road to Nunavut: the Progress of the Eastern Arctic Inuit Since the Second World War. Kingston, Ont.: McGill-Queen's University Press.

A description of the transformation of the Inuit of the eastern Canadian arctic from a hunting and trapping society to a sedentary population tied to the economy of southern Canada and striving for self-government.

1-25   Elliot, J. L. (1984, September). Emerging Ethnic Nationalism in the Canadian Northwest Territories. Canadian Review of Studies in Nationalism, 11(2), 231-244.

This essay argues that ethnicity is a basis of sociality irreducible to any other, and that it is the principle of social organization that best elucidates the native nationalism emerging in the Canadian Arctic, in Nunavut, and Denendeh.

1-26   An Enabling Agreement Between the Government of Canada and the Government of the Northwest Territories Respecting Oil and Gas Resource Management and Revenues = Entente Permettant au Gouvernement du Canada de Conclure Avec le Gouvernement des Territoires du Nord-Quest L'accord Concernant la Gestion des Ressources Petrolieres et Gazieres et les Recettes Connexes. (1988). Yellowknife, N.W.T.: Government of the Northwest Territories.

Tabled document no. 2-88(2) tabled on October 13, 1988. Text of the Northern Accord under which the federal government of Canada agrees to the phased transfer to the Government of the Northwest Territories of the administrative and legislative powers to manage onshore oil and gas resources. Caption title: Northern Accord agreement-in-principle.

1-27   The Evolution of Public Governments in the North and the Implications For Aboriginal Peoples. (1993). Ottawa, Ont.: Indian and Northern Affairs Canada.

This paper is intended to provide a historical perspective of the evolution of public government in the Yukon and Northwest Territories, and describes the relationships between Aboriginal organizations and the federal and territorial governments as these have developed over the last century in Canada, including Nunavut and other regional and local government models.

1-28   The Federal Comprehensive Claims Policy. (1987, June). Building Blocks, (7), 5-6.

Summary of background, purpose and objectives, and scope of negotiations of the new federal claims policy, including extinguishment.

1-29 Fenge, T. A. (1979). Land Use Programs in Canada: Northwest Territories. Ottawa, Ont.: Environment Canada, Lands Directorate.

Roles of the federal and territorial agencies engaged in land use planning and/or land management in the N.W.T. are outlined and the pertinent legislation is identified and discussed. Concerns and issues regarding land use and land management are also detailed.

1-30 Fenge, T. A., & Rees, W. E. (1987). Hinterland or Homeland? : Land-Use Planning in Northern Canada. Ottawa, Ont.: Canadian Arctic Resources Committee.

Describes the history of planning in northern Canada, implementation of the 1981 federal land use policy, and specific problems in the Yukon and the N.W.T. Includes chapters on land use planning and the Tungavik Federation of Nunavut landclaim, the problems of oil and gas extraction from the Beaufort Sea- Mackenzie Delta region and land use planning in northern Quebec.

1-31 Franks, C. E. S. (1987). Public Administration Questions Relating to Aboriginal Self-Government. Aboriginal Peoples and Constitutional Reform Background Paper, 12. Kingston, Ont.: Queen's University, Institute of Intergovernmental Relations.

Examines three aspects of the issues to be resolved to make aboriginal self-government a concrete reality. They are: the special features of an "aboriginal" as opposed to another kind of government; the question of "public" aspects of aboriginal self-government, its functions, etc.; administrative questions such as financing, policy-making and personnel administration. Identifies some of the problems and indicates what issues must be addressed in the process of establishing aboriginal self-government and self-administration.

1-32 Funston, B. W. (1980). The Northwest Territories in Canadian Federalism 1963-79. Masters Thesis, Scott Polar Research Institute, Cambridge, England.

Examines political and constitutional developments in the N.W.T. in the context of federal-provincial relations, petroleum resource development, and native people's proposals for administrative restructuring between 1963 and 1979.

1-33 Gatner, J. A. (1984). Division of Northwest Territories: A Background Paper For Parliamentarians. Ottawa, Ont.: Library of Parliament. Research Branch.

Recounts chronologically the divisions of the N.W.T., from the creation of Manitoba in 1870 to the unresolved boundary issue of Nunavut in 1984.

1-34 GNWT Transfer Policy. (1988). Yellowknife, N.W.T.: Government of the Northwest Territories .

Tabled document no. 91-88(1) tabled on March 7, 1988. This document outlines the objectives of devolution of decision-making and delivery of services from the territorial and federal governments, to communities in the Northwest Territories, together with definitions and outlines of policy.

1-35   Graham, K. A., Brown, S., McAllister, A. B., & Wojciechowski, M. J. (1984). A Climate for Change: Alternatives for the Central and Eastern Arctic. Eastern Arctic Study Series. Kingston, Ont.: Queen's University, Centre for Resource Studies: Institute of Local Government.

Final report of the Eastern Arctic Study to develop and assess alternative approaches to political development and landclaims settlement in Canada's central and eastern Arctic. Describes the trends in political development, landclaims and industrial development in the N.W.T.

1-36   Graham, K. A., & McAllister, A. B. (1981). The Inuit Land Claim, Constitutional Development, and Local Government Reform in the Northwest Territories: an Overview. Kingston, Ont.: Institute of Local Government and Centre for Resource Studies, Queen's University.

Provides basic information on the landclaim of the Inuit Tapirisat of Canada, and on recent constitutional and local government changes in the Northwest Territories.

1-37   Hawkes, D. C. (1985). Negotiating Aboriginal Self-Government. In P. M. Leslie (Editor), Canada: the State of the Federation, (pp. 151-172). Kingston, Ont.: Queen's University.

An examination of recent negotiations on aboriginal self-government, concentrating analysis on developments which have occurred since the election of the Progressive Conservative federal government in September 1984.

1-38   Holmes, D. (1990, July). Waiting On the Porch. Arctic Circle, 1(1), 50-53.

Commentary of northern opinion on the political changes needed in the north in relation to the Meech Lake Accord.

1-39   Indian and Inuit Education. (1990). Information Sheet (Canada. Indian and Northern Affairs Canada), 1990:5. Ottawa, Ont.: Indian and Northern Affairs Canada.

Outlines the mandate for and jurisdiction of education for Indians and Inuit in Canada, including costs and devolution of powers to local administrations.

1-40   Indian Chiefs of Alberta (1970). Citizens Plus: a Presentation to Right Honourable P.E. Trudeau, June 4, 1970. Edmonton, Alta.: Indian Association of Alberta.

Known as the Red Paper. In opposition to the "Statement of the Government of Canada on Indian Policy 1969" (White Paper), Alberta Indian chiefs presented several options to the federal government (Red Paper).

1-41   Irwin, C. (1989). <u>Lords of the Arctic: Wards of the State: the Growing Inuit Population, Arctic Resettlement and Their Effects on Social and Economic Change</u>. Halifax, N.S.: Dalhousie University, Dept. of Sociology and Social Anthropology.

Attempts to describe the social and economic changes brought about by the resettlement of Inuit into villages in the late 1950's and early 1960's and by the growth of the Inuit population in the Canadian Arctic.

1-42   Irwin, C., & Malone, M. (1989). Lords of the Arctic: Wards of the State: the Growing Inuit Population, Arctic Resettlement, and Their Effects on Social and Economic Change: A Summary Report. <u>Northern Perspectives</u>, 17(1), 1-20.

Contains shortened version of Irwin's "Lords of the Arctic" report on the future of the Inuit, together with responses on behalf of the Government of N.W.T. and the Tungavik Federation of Nunavut and Irwin's reply to these responses.

1-43   <u>Joint Statement by the Honourable Tony Penikett, Government Leader, Government of Yukon and the Honourable Dennis Patterson, Deputy Government Leader, Government of the Northwest Territories on Federal Comprehensive Claims Policy</u>. (1986). Yellowknife, N.W.T.: NWT Legislature.

Tabled Document no. 77-86 tabled on June 25, 1986. Both governments support the new federal comprehensive claims policy based on the Coolican Task Force Report.

1-44   Jull, P. (1988, June). Building Nunavut: A Story of Inuit Self-Government. <u>Northern Review</u>, (1), 59-72.

Outlines the history of the concept of Nunavut, a self-governing territory in the eastern and northern portions of the Northwest Territories.

1-45   Jull, P. (1991). Canada's Northwest Territories: Constitutional Development and Aboriginal Rights. In P. Jull, & S. Roberts (Editors), <u>The Challenge of Northern Regions</u>, (pp. 43-64). Australia: North Australis Research Unit, Australian National University.

Provides a chronology of federal and territorial government actions and attitudes as they relate to administration of the N.W.T. in the period ranging from postwar era until 1990. The growth of the proposal for a Nunavut government is also detailed, particularly for the post-1979 period.

1-46   Jull, P. (1987, March). Northern Canada and Northern Peoples: Some Comparative Experiences. <u>IWGIA Document</u>, (58), 131- 141.

Discussion of the experiences of Inuit, Dene and Metis groups in the Northwest Territories and Quebec, in negotiating with the Federal Government in settlement of landclaims.

1-47   Jull, P. (1983). <u>Nunavurt = Nunavut</u>. Frobisher Bay, N.W.T.: Nunavut
        Constitutional Forum.

        Details life of northern Canadian Inuit especially since World War II, to give
        a clearer understanding of the political evolution of the area, and the
        establishment of a Nunavut government.

1-48   Jull, P. (1986). <u>Politics, Development and Conservation in the International
        North</u>. CARC Policy Paper, 2. Ottawa, Ont.: Canadian Arctic Resources
        Committee.

        Author asserts that conservation is the fundamental issue of politics in
        northern areas. He describes the political questions that arise from conflicts
        between conservation and development in the proposed Nunavut territory of
        northern Canada, in Alaska and in northern Norway.

1-49   Jull, P. (1984). <u>Self-government for Northern Peoples: Canada and the
        Circumpolar Story: A Report to the Government of the Northwest
        Territories...</u> Yellowknife, N.W.T.: Aboriginal Rights and Constitutional
        Development Secretariat.

        A report to the Government of the N.W.T. giving a clear and concise
        overview of the issues in political development for northern peoples around
        the circumpolar world. Presents some useful insights into the various
        political developments and initiatives that are of interest and relevance to the
        N.W.T.

1-50   Key Components of a New Federal Policy for Comprehensive Land Claims.
        (1987, January). <u>Northern Perspectives</u>, 15(1), 16- 17.

        The Report of the Task Force to Review Comprehensive Claims Policy,
        released in March 1986, recommends fundamental changes to current
        federal policy. These briefing notes outline the key elements that aboriginal
        peoples feel must be addressed in the new policy.

1-51   MacLachlan, L. J. (1992, March). Comprehensive Aboriginal Claims in the
        N.W.T. <u>Information North</u>, 18(1), 1-8.

        Provides overview of landclaims, of policy of Canadian government
        towards those claims in the Northwest Territories, current status, and
        resource management institutions that will be created as direct result of
        settlement.

1-52   MacPherson, S. (1982). <u>Local Government in the Northwest Territories</u>.
        Ottawa, Ont.: Carleton University, Dept. of Political Science.

        Examines local government in the N.W.T and the various proposals for
        change. Includes discussion of native organizations.

1-53   McKnight, B. (1986). <u>Speaking Notes For the Honourable Bill McKnight,</u>
        <u>Minister of Indian Affairs and Northern Development on Comprehensive</u>
        <u>Claims Policy: December 18, 1986.</u> Ottawa, Ont.: Indian and Northern
        Affairs Canada.

        Text of speech to the House of Commons describing the major elements in
        a new federal government policy on comprehensive claims "Living Treaties,
        Lasting Agreements" (Coolican Report).

1-54   McNeil, K. (1982). <u>Native Claims in Rupert's Land and the North-Western</u>
        <u>Territory: Canada's Constitutional Obligations.</u> Studies in Aboriginal
        Rights, 5. Saskatoon, Sask.: University of Saskatchewan, Native Law
        Centre.

        An examination of the nature and extent of the obligation of the Canadian
        government to settle the aboriginal landclaims in Rupert's Land and the
        North-Western Territory from the orders transferring the land in 1870.

1-55   Merritt, J. A. (1984). Background Paper: A Review of Federal Land-Claims
        Policy. In <u>National and Regional Interests in the North: Third National</u>
        <u>Workshop on People, Resources, and the Environment North of 60,</u>
        <u>Yellowknife, N.W.T. 1-3 June 1983</u>, (pp. 71-86). Ottawa, Ont.: Canadian
        Arctic Resources Committee.

        Summary and critique of "In All Fairness", the Federal Government position
        on native landclaims, including a discussion of the consequences of flexible
        response, suggestions for improvement in the negotiating process, and
        changes in federal expectations for native peoples.

1-56   Merritt, J. A. (1987, January). In Search of Common Ground: Ottawa Rethinks
        Its Approach to Comprehensive Claims. <u>Northern Perspectives</u>, 15(1), 1-4.

        The article offers background to the Coolican report, and an over-all
        summary of the direction of the report.

1-57   Morissest, J. (1981, June). The Aboriginal Nationhood, The Northern Challenge
        and the Construction of Canadian Unity. <u>Queen's Quarterly</u>, 237-249.

        Discussion of the "colonial" attitude of central government in Canada
        towards the north and of all levels of government towards aboriginal
        peoples, and of the southern belief that inclusion of the north will create and
        complete Canadian unity.

1-58   Morrison, W. R. (1985). <u>A Survey of the History and Claims of the Native</u>
        <u>Peoples of Northern Canada</u>. Ottawa, Ont.: Department of Indian Affairs
        and Northern Development.

        Includes chapters on the Yukon, Mackenzie, Nunavut, northern Quebec
        and Labrador landclaims.

1-59   Morrison, W. R. (1984). <u>Under the Flag: Canadian Sovereignty and the Native</u> <u>People in Northern Canada</u>. Ottawa, Ont.: Department of Indian and Northern Affairs and Northern Development, Treaties and Historical Research Centre.

Study of the extension of sovereignty to Yukon, Hudson Bay and the western, central and eastern arctic between 1895 and 1925. Includes an examination of the concepts of sovereignty and native title.

1-60   Moss, W. (1990). <u>Aboriginal Land Claims Issues</u>. Background Paper. (Canada. Library of Parliament Research Branch), BP- 237E. Ottawa, Ont.: Library of Parliament, Research Branch.

This paper describes specific claims policy, comprehensive claims policy, and the issues of claims policy such as distinguishing between specific and comprehensive claims, conflicts of interest, extinguishment of aboriginal title, aboriginal title "superseded by law" and exclusion of self-government agreements from landclaims agreements.

1-61   <u>Northern Political and Economic Policy Framework</u>. (1989). Information Sheet (Canada. Indian and Northern Affairs Canada), 1989:23. Ottawa, Ont.: Indian and Northern Affairs Canada.

Outline of the four components of the Northern Political and Economic Policy Framework (Northern Framework) for the activities of the Federal Government in the Northwest Territories and Yukon: devolution, landclaims, economic development and Arctic sovereignty.

1-62   Northwest Territories. Commission for Constitutional Development (1992). <u>Phase 1 Report: Working Toward a Common Future</u>. Yellowknife, N.W.T.: s.n.

This study originated with the Committee of Political Leaders of the western Northwest Territories who established the Commission for Constitutional Development, which held public hearings on government of the proposed New Western Territory. The report includes proposals for name, geographic area, First People' rights, orders of government, possible districts, institutions and a draft constitution.

1-63   Northwest Territories Executive Council (1991). <u>A Position Paper on Political</u> <u>and Constitutional Development Presented by the Executive Council,</u> <u>Government of the Northwest Territories to the Legislative Assembly</u>. Yellowknife, N.W.T.: Government of the Northwest Territories.

Statement of the views of the Executive Council of the Government of the Northwest Territories on current constitutional issues to be settled before 1997: landclaims, division (Nunavut and a new region), Northern Accord, devolution of land and water regulation, constitutional development, self-government, national issues, and provincial status.

1-64   Northwest Territories Government (1986). A Sessional Paper: Political and
        Constitutional Development in the Northwest Territories. Yellowknife,
        N.W.T.: Northwest Territories. Legislative Assembly.

        Tabled document no. 67-86(1) tabled on June 16, 1986. Outlines the
        N.W.T. government's political and constitutional objectives, principles, and
        the current political and constitutional issues which revolve around division,
        devolution, and settlement of claims.

1-65   Northwest Territories Legislative Assembly (1992). Report of the Special
        Committee on Constitutional Reform on the Multilateral Meetings on the
        Constitution and First Ministers Aboriginal Leaders Conferences on the
        Constitution. Yellowknife, N.W.T.: Northwest Territories Legislative
        Assembly.

        Committee report no. 18-12(2) tabled on September 16, 1992. This report
        summarizes the course of various meetings on reform of the Constitution of
        Canada including the Multilateral Meetings on the Constitution (MMCs)
        and the Pearson Accord. Includes the status of the Northwest Territories,
        aboriginal peoples and texts of various proposals for change.

1-66   Northwest Territories. Minister for Aboriginal Rights and Constitutional
        Development (1981). Discussion Paper on Political and Constitutional
        Development in the Northwest Territories. Yellowknife, N.W.T.: Northwest
        Territories. Minister for Aboriginal Rights and Constitutional Development.

        Presents background information on the Northwest Territories
        Government, and discusses the division of federal/territorial powers.

1-67   Northwest Territories. Project to Review the Operations and Structure of
        Northern Government (1991). Strength at Two Levels: Report of the
        Project To Review the Operations and Structure of Northern Government.
        Yellowknife, N.W.T.: Financial Management Board.

        Tabled document no. 03-12(1) tabled on December 9, 1991. This report
        attempts to provide a blueprint for government organizational and program
        change over the next ten years in the Northwest Territories, including
        recommendations relating to devolution of powers to community level, re-
        thinking of purposes and means of service delivery and an appendix setting
        out detailed plans and procedures to implement change.

1-68   Nunavut Territory, Canada. (1991). In P. Jull, The Politics of Northern
        Frontiers: In Australia, Canada and Other "First World" Countries, (pp. 16-20).
        Australia: North Australia Research Unit Australian National University.

        A summary of the political situation in the Northwest Territories,
        specifically Nunavut, and history of the landclaim negotiations and their
        significance, as compared to Australia and other countries.

1-69   O'Malley, M. (1976). <u>The Past and Future Land: An Account of the Berger Inquiry Into the Mackenzie Valley Pipeline</u>. Toronto, Ont.: Peter Martin Associates Limited.

Discussion of the land and title of the Mackenzie Valley region of the Northwest Territories and the changes that could result from construction of the proposed pipeline.

1-70   Peters, E. J. (1986) <u>Aboriginal Self-Government in Canada: a Bibliography 1986</u>. Kingston, Ont.: Queen's University, Institute of Intergovernmental Relations.

Almost 700 references listed alphabetically by author in five parts: I. General papers. II. The First Ministers' Conferences on Aboriginal Constitutional matters: papers and public documents. III. Federal and provincial approaches to aboriginal self-government. IV. Existing self-government agreements and related papers. V. Aboriginal peoples' approaches to self-government (including N.W.T. and Yukon).

1-71   <u>Political Change North of 60</u>. (1988). Current Issue Review, 88-3E. Ottawa, Ont.: Library of Parliament, Research Branch.

Discusses chronologically the political and administrative changes in the Yukon and Northwest Territories, including proposals to divide the Northwest Territories into Nunavut and Denendeh, and the 1987 Meech Lake Accord. Updated periodically.

1-72   <u>Recent Developments on National Constitutional Reform</u>. (1992). Yellowknife, N.W.T.: Government of the Northwest Territories.

This speech by the Minister of Intergovernmental and Aboriginal Affairs, Northwest Territories, announces the full participation of aboriginal and territorial delegates in discussions on the constitution of Canada, following publication of the report of the Joint Parliamentary Committee on a renewed Canada.

1-73   Robertson, G. (1989). The Human Foundation for Peace and Security in the Arctic. In <u>The Arctic: Choices for Peace and Security</u>, (pp. 87-92). West Vancouver, B.C.: Gordon Soules .

Paper given at a conference held March 18-19, 1989, in Edmonton, Alberta. Author argues that there can be no successful international Arctic policy without self-reliant, self-respecting and self-directing population in the Canadian Arctic. Supports establishment of Nunavut and Denendeh.

1-74   Robertson, G. (1988). <u>New Directions North of 60</u>. Yellowknife, N.W.T.: Government of the Northwest Territories.

This paper discusses possible development of new constitutional and governmental structures in the Northwest Territories following the agreement signed in Iqaluit in 1987 between the Western Constitutional

Forum (Indian and Metis groups living in the western part of the Northwest Territories) and the Nunavut Constitutional Forum (Inuit and others living in the eastern Arctic).

1-75   Robertson, G. (1985). Northern Provinces: A Mistaken Goal. Montreal, Que.: Institute for Research on Public Policy.

Written by a former Commissioner of the Northwest Territories. This book suggests that if provincial status is attained by N.W.T. and Yukon, it would create many problems. Instead, he suggests the establishment of autonomous federal territories.

1-76   Robertson, G. (1987). Political Development for the Northern Future. s.l.: s.n.

Argues that provincial status will not be a feasible solution for future political development in the north. Calls for the establishment of Nunavut and full self-government for the remaining territories with special constitutional protections for the cultural security of the aboriginal peoples.

1-77   Schmitz, G. (1986). Aboriginal Rights and Land Claims. Current Issue Review, 82-9E. Ottawa, Ont.: Library of Parliament.

Traces the history and current status of the recognition of aboriginal rights and landclaims in Canada. Includes a chronology (1969-86) of the present negotiations.

1-78   Schmitz, G., & Terry, J. (1988). Political Change North of 60. Current Issue Review, 88-3E. Ottawa, Ont.: Library of Parliament, Research Branch.

Discusses chronologically the political and administrative changes in the Yukon and Northwest Territories, including proposals to divide the Northwest Territories into Nunavut and Denendeh, and the 1987 Meech Lake Accord.

1-79   Schwartz, B. (1985). First Principles: Constitutional Reform With Respect to the Aboriginal Peoples of Canada, 1982- 1984. Aboriginal Peoples and Constitutional Reform. Background Paper, 6. Kingston, Ont.: Queen's University, Institute of Intergovernmental Relations.

Study of constitutional reform with respect to aboriginal peoples in Canada, from patriation of the Constitution in 1982 to the First Ministers' Conferences on Constitutional Aboriginal Matters in 1983 and 1984.

1-80   Seize the Day: a Report to the Legislative Assembly on Political and Constitutional Development in the Northwest Territories, Government of the N.W.T., October 27, 1989. (1989). Yellowknife, N.W.T.: Government of the Northwest Territories.

Tabled document no.18-89(2) tabled on October 27, 1989. This report outlines the issues involved in the transfer of power from the Federal Government to the Government of the Northwest Territories and in

devolution of responsibility for delivery of services from the Territorial
Government to the communities, in the context of Canadian constitutional
change.

1-81   Smith, G. W. (1952). The Historical and Legal Background of Canada's Arctic
        Claims. Doctoral Dissertation, Columbia University, New York, N.Y.

        Examines Canada's territorial claims in the north polar region and efforts to
        establish sovereignty throughout the northern territories.

1-82   Task Force to Review Comprehensive Claims Policy (1985). Living Treaties:
        Lasting Agreements: Report of the Task Force to Review Comprehensive
        Claims Policy. Ottawa, Ont.: Department of Indian Affairs and Northern
        Development.

        Chairman: Murray Coolican. Traces the background of aboriginal claims
        agreements in Canadian history and law and analyses the new constitutional
        context in which contemporary landclaims policy must be made. Includes
        sections on self-government and northern political development. Known as
        the "Coolican Report".

1-83   TFN Profile. (Revised) (1985). Ottawa, Ontario: Tungavik Federation of
        Nunavut.

        Outline of the aims, organization, functions and membership of the
        Tungavik Federation of Nunavut.

1-84   Tungavik Federation of Nunavut (TFN) Comprehensive Claim: Northwest
        Territories. (1989). Information Sheet (Canada. Indian and Northern
        Affairs Canada), 1989:8. Ottawa, Ont.: Indian and Northern Affairs Canada.

        Brief background and chronology of the landclaim by the Tungavik
        Federation of Nunavut representing Inuit residents of the N.W.T.

1-85   Tungavik Federation of Nunavut (TFN) Comprehensive Claim: Northwest
        Territories. (1990). Information Sheet (Canada. Indian and Northern
        Affairs Canada), 1990:8. Ottawa, Ont.: Indian and Northern Affairs Canada.

        Brief background and chronology of the landclaim by the Tungavik
        Federation of Nunavut representing Inuit residents of the Northwest
        Territories.

1-86   Viewpoint North: Constitutional Development in the N.W.T.: a Discussion.
        (1985, March). Information North, (1), 2-6.

        In January 1985, the Constitutional Alliance of the Northwest Territories
        reached a tentative agreement on a boundary for division of the Territories
        into two separate northern territories. The Alliance comprises the Western
        Constitutional Forum (WCF) and Nunavut (eastern) Constitutional Forum
        (NCF).

1-87   Weller, G. R. (1990). Devolution, Regionalism and Division of the Northwest
        Territories. In G. Dacks (Editor), <u>Devolution and Constitutional
        Development in the Canadian North</u>, (pp. 317-334). Ottawa, Ont.: Carleton
        University Press.

        Discusses implications of power transfer from Canadian federal government
        to government of the Northwest Territories for enhancement of regional
        administrative structure and possible division of N.W.T.

1-88   Whittington, M. S. (1985). <u>The North</u>. The Collected Research Studies/Royal
        Commission on the Economic Union and Development Prospects for
        Canada, 72. Toronto, Ont.: University of Toronto Press.

        One of a series commissioned as part of the research program of the Royal
        Commission on the Economic Union and Development Prospects for
        Canada. Contains a series of essays on political and economic development
        in the Northwest Territories and Yukon including sovereignty, constitutional
        development, landclaims, and environmental perspectives.

1-89   Zlotkin, N. K. (1983). <u>Unfinished Business: Aboriginal Peoples and the 1983
        Constitutional Conference</u>. Institute of Intergovernmental Relations.
        Discussion Paper, 15. Kingston, Ont.: Queen's University.

        Discussion paper providing a detailed guide through the issues facing the
        conference. Explores the legal and juridical precedents in the pre-1982
        constitutional treatment of natives and describes the participation of
        aboriginal groups in the negotiations leading to the Constitution Act, 1982.

SECTION 2: HISTORICAL TO 1963

2-1   Canada. Dept. of Indian Affairs and Northern Development (1969). <u>Statement of
        the Government of Canada on Indian Policy 1969</u>. Ottawa, Ont.: Queen's
        Printer.

        Known as the White Paper. Presented to the first session of the 28th
        Parliament by the Honourable Jean Chretien, Minister of Indian Affairs and
        Northern Development. Proposed abolition of the Department of Indian
        Affairs and Northern Development and changes to status of Indians.

2-2   Canada. Royal Commission to Investigate the Unfilled Provisions of Treaties 8
        and 11 As They Apply to the Indians of the Mackenzie District (1959).
        <u>Report of the Commission Appointed to Investigate the Unfulfilled
        Provisions of Treaties 8 and 11 as They Apply to the Indians of the
        Mackenzie Valley</u>. s.l.: s.n.

        Report of the study made of Treaties 8 and 11 to determine whether all
        aspects of the treaties had been implemented and whether the federal
        government had met its obligations to the Indians affected. (Known as the
        "Nelson Commission".)

2-3   Coates, K. S., & Morrison, William R. (1986). Treaty Research Report: Treaty
        Eleven (1921). Ottawa, Ont.: Indian Affairs and Northern Development.

        This account of the negotiations and signing of Treaty Eleven covering the
        Indians of the Mackenzie Valley, Northwest Territories, includes a map of
        the treaty area, text of the treaty, list of bands and reserves, and a
        bibliography of primary and secondary sources.

2-4   Evolution of the Boundaries of the Northwest Territories. (1992, March).
        Nunavut, 11(2), 30-31.

        Maps and brief history of changes in the boundaries of the Northwest
        Territories from 1867 to 1967.

2-5   Morrison, W. R. (1984). Under the Flag: Canadian Sovereignty and the Native
        People in Northern Canada. Ottawa, Ont.: Department of Indian and
        Northern Affairs and Northern Development, Treaties and Historical
        Research Centre.

        Study of the extension of sovereignty to Yukon, Hudson Bay and the
        western, central and eastern arctic between 1895 and 1925. Includes an
        examination of the concepts of sovereignty and native life.

2-6   Narvey, K. M. (1973). The Royal Proclamation of 7 October 1763, the Common
        Law, and Native Rights to Land Within the Territory Granted to the
        Hudson's Bay Company. Saskatchewan Law Review, 38, 123-233.

        This examination of the implications the Royal Proclamation of 1763
        concludes that it does apply to territory later granted to the Hudson's Bay
        Company, in the absence of other legislation, and that common law rights
        should apply to native peoples in areas never ceded to the Crown.

2-7   Smith, G. W. (1952). The Historical and Legal Background of Canada's Arctic
        Claims. Doctoral Dissertation, Columbia University, New York, N.Y.

        Examines Canada's territorial claims in the north polar region and efforts to
        establish sovereignty throughout the northern territories.

2-8   Treaty No. 11 (June 27, 1921) and Adhesion (July 17, 1922) With Reports, Etc.
        (1967). Ottawa, Ont.: Queen's Printer.

        Report of the Commissioner for Treaty No. 11 (1921), text of the Treaty
        and map of the area covered (Mackenzie Valley, Northwest Territories).

2-9   Treaty No. 8 Made June 21, 1899, and Adhesions, Reports, Etc. (1957).
        Ottawa, Ont.: Queen's Printer.

        Reports of the Commissioner for Treaty No. 8 (1899) text of the Treaty
        and map of the area covered (part of northern British Columbia, part of the
        present northern Alberta, part of the present northern Saskatchewan, and an
        area of the present Northwest Territories southeast of Great Slave Lake).

SECTION 3: HISTORICAL 1964 - 1982

3-1   The 1982 Plebiscite. (1982, March). Nunavut, 11(2), 24.

       Summary of the 1982 plebiscite on whether the Northwest Territories
       should be divided.

3-2   Abele, F., & Dickerson, M. O. (1986). The 1982 Plebiscite On Division of the
       Northwest Territories: Regional Government and Federal Policy. Canadian
       Public Policy/Analyse de Politiques, 11(1), 1-15.

       The authors contend that the plebiscite results, particularly in Inuit
       communities in the eastern arctic, are consistent with broad goals of native
       groups - namely establishing government in smaller territories, preserving
       cultural identity, and generally assuming greater control of their own affairs.

3-3   Amagoalik, J. (1976, March). The Proposal For Inuit Land Claims. Inuit Today,
       5(3), 22-32.

       Outline and discussion of the rationale for and terms of the Inuit Tapirisat
       proposal for landclaims, presented to the Federal Government in 1975,
       asking for creation of Nunavut. (Continued in "Inuit Today" v.5, no. 4,
       April 1976. pp. 26-33.)

3-4   Amys, J. H. (1981, September). Nunavut. The Law Society Gazette, 15(3),
       270-277.

       Review of the submission "Parnagujuk" made by the Inuit Tapirisat of
       Canada to the federal government, for separation of Nunavut from the
       Northwest Territories, as a reasoned argument for the granting of a northern
       equivalent of a provincial and municipal mandate to decide regional and
       local affairs.

3-5   Archaeology Provisions of an Agreement-in-Principle. (1982). Rankin Inlet,
       N.W.T.: Tungavik Federation of Nunavut.

       Draft of proposed clauses of the Nunavut Agreement relating to the
       archaeological record of the Inuit.

3-6   Bayly, J. U. (1976). COPE-ITC Submissions. Yellowknife, N.W.T.: Brand.

       Summary of argument, terms and conditions, and recommendations
       proposed by Committee for Original Peoples' Entitlement (COPE) and Inuit
       Tapirisat of Canada (ITC) to Mackenzie Valley Pipeline Inquiry. Position
       of Inuvialuit, as determined by COPE visits to Inuit communities in northern
       Canada, is no pipeline before landclaims are settled.

3-7   Bickenbach, J. E. (1980). The Baker Lake Case: a Partial Recognition of Inuit
       Aboriginal Title. University of Toronto Faculty of Law Review, 38, 232-
       249.

Discussion of the Baker Lake case (1980) in which the Inuit of the area sought restraint of mining activities that they alleged disrupted caribou hunting and therefore violated aboriginal rights. The judgment refused the restraint but held that the area was subject to the aboriginal right and title to hunt and fish.

3-8   Boreal Institute for Northern Studies (1975). Canadian Arctic Renewal Resource Mapping Project. Inuit Tapirisat of Canada, Renewable Resources Project. London, Ont., Waterloo, Ont.: University of Western Ontario and University of Waterloo.

A project to provide an easily understood map series and accompanying explanatory text to assist the Inuit in preparing landclaims, using published biological information.

3-9   Brown, M. P. S., Graham, K. A., & Wojciechowski, M. J. Eastern Arctic Study Case Study Series: Beaufort Sea Oil and Gas Development. (1985). Kingston, Ont.: Centre for Resource Studies, Queen's University.

The overall objective of the Eastern Arctic Study was to examine the implications of constitutional development and of landclaims for local government and for mineral development in one particular landclaim area, that of the Inuit Tapirisat of Canada. The basic purpose of these [EAS case studies] is to examine specific instances of past industry/community and other government interaction concerning industrial development.

3-10   Cairns, R. (1982). Western Arctic Constitutional Conference. North, 29(1), 2-5.

Conference on government of Northwest Territories and native rights, January 1982, at which Dene/Metis groups and territorial and federal officials discussed the Denendeh and Nunavut claims.

3-11   Canada. Privy Council, & Drury, C. M. (1979). Constitutional Development in the Northwest Territories: Report of the Special Representative. Hull, Que.: Supply and Services.

(Known as the Drury Report.) This document examines the constitutional situation of the N.W.T. including federal jurisdictional responsibilities and factors affecting changes to territorial status. Issues of native claims, social development and public finances are identified as major impediments to local political development. Public concerns expressed in meetings and hearings throughout the north are stated. A process leading to eventual constitutional changes in the N.W.T., based on resolution of other problems first, is suggested.

3-12   Central Arctic Regional Government Proposal Within Nunavut Government. (1980). Yellowknife, N.W.T.: Kitikmeot Inuit Association.

Discussion paper on concerns of Inuit of the central Arctic (Kitikmeot) on matters to be included in a landclaims agreement.

3-13   <u>Central Arctic Regional Land Claims Proposal for Social, Educational Self-Determination</u>. (1979). Resolute Bay, N.W.T.: Kitikmeot Inuit Association.

Statement of concerns by Inuit of the central Arctic (Kitikmeot) on social and educational matters to be included in a landclaims settlement.

3-14   Cumming, P. A. (1973). Inuit Hunting Rights in the Northwest Territories. <u>Saskatchewan Law Review</u>, 38, 252-323.

This paper emphasizes the importance of enhancing and protecting Inuit hunting rights as being special rights of a native people within Canadian society, including the present attitude of the Government of the Northwest Territories, history of legislation, and effects of the Canadian Bill of Rights.

3-15   Cumming, P. A. (1982, June). Native Peoples and Aboriginal Rights. <u>North</u>, 29(2), 12-16.

This article discusses the question of Arctic native peoples and their landclaims through an examination of the COPE Agreement-in-Principle signed with the Inuvialuit of the Western Arctic region of the Northwest Territories and a historical account of treaties and current landclaim issues.

3-16   <u>Dene Rights: Supporting Research and Documents</u>. (1976). Yellowknife, N.W.T.: Indian Brotherhood of the Northwest Territories.

Material to support Dene landclaims in the Mackenzie Valley, Northwest Territories, including the legal and constitutional basis, the Dene Declaration and an evaluation of the Alaska Claims Settlement Act.

3-17   Dickerson, M. O. (1982). Commentary: the Drury Report and Political Development in the N.W.T. <u>Arctic</u>, 35(4), 457-464.

Examination of the report "Constitutional Development in the Northwest Territories," by C.M. Drury, 1979.

3-18   Drury, C. M. (1979). <u>Constitutional Development in the Northwest Territories</u>. Hull, Que.: Supply and Services.

This federal report examines the constitutional situation of the N.W.T. including federal jurisdictional responsibilities and factors affecting changes to territorial status. Issues of native claims, social development and public finances are identified as major impediments to local political development.

3-19   Elliott, D. W. (1980). Baker Lake and the Concept of Aboriginal Title. <u>Osgoode Hall Law Journal</u>, 18, 653-663.

This examination of the Baker Lake case of 1980 compares its conclusions on aboriginal rights to those in the Calder decision (1973).

3-20   Federal Government May Try to Back Out of Wildlife Deal. (1982, June 15).
        Nunavut Newsletter, (1), 1-2.

        Discussion of possibility of changes to the Nunavut Wildlife Agreement-in-
        Principle initialed in 1981.

3-21   Funston, B. W. (1982). The Northwest Territories and Its Future Constitutional
        and Political Development: An Examination of the Drury Report. Polar
        Record, 21(131), 117-125.

        Examination of the Report of the Special Representative on Constitutional
        Development in the Northwest Territories, in light of the Canadian
        Constitution Act of 1982.

3-22   Gedalof, R. (1981, February). Hot Issues in a Cold Land. Interface, 4(1), 52-54.

        The author outlines the progress made by the Inuit in the last 50 years
        towards political maturity, self-government, and the eventual full provincial
        status for Nunavut.

3-23   Gribbons, C. (1976, December). Important Changes to the Nunavut Claim.
        C.A.S.N.P. Bulletin, 17(3), 13-15.

        Discussion of the revised landclaim made by the Inuit Tapirisat of Canada
        (ITC) to ensure a Nunavut government with more autonomy than the
        traditional territorial type of administration.

3-24   Hall, N. A. (1981, July). Nunavut Affairs Planning Office. Inuit Today, (9), 18.

        Approval for the establishment of a Nunavut Affairs Planning Office
        (NAPO) by the Board of Directors of Inuit Tapirisat of Canada (ITC), to
        provide information on Nunavut and the landclaims settlement.

3-25   Hall, N. A. (1981, November). Nunavut Land Claims - Report. Inuit Today,
        (9), 64-74.

        Summary of recent progress on landclaims, the negotiations on wildlife
        harvesting and game management, and organization of a new governing
        body to take over the work of Nunavut Affairs Planning Office (NAPO).

3-26   Harvesting. (1982, July). Nunavut Newsletter, (2), 9.

        Announcement of a Nunavut Wildlife Harvesting Study, to begin within two
        years after the Final Agreement is signed.

3-27   Herchmer, H. (1980). Caribou Eskimos v. the Canadian Legal System. Northern
        Perspectives, 8(3), 2-8.

        Background to Baker Lake Eskimos' court action in 1979 to protect their
        land from mining companies and clarify issue of aboriginal rights.

3-28   Herchmer, H. L. (1980, June). The Twelfth Province. Canadian Heritage, 22-24.

Brief review of "southern" public attitudes to the Inuit and the idea of
Nunavut.

3-29   Hollo, G. (1981, July). How Do We Cross The River? Inuit Today, (9), 28,32.

Discussion of progress at the second Nunavut Leadership Workshop, Baker
Lake, N.W.T., 1981, in training Inuit leaders.

3-30   The Honourable C. M. Drury's Report on Constitutional Development in the
Northwest Territories: Press Release. (1980). Ottawa, Ont.: Special
Representative For Constitutional Development in the Northwest
Territories.

Summary of the Drury Report recommending against division of the
Northwest Territories together with response from Inuit Tapirisat of Canada
and summary of proposed political development of Nunavut.

3-31   Institute of Local Government and Centre for Resource Studies (1980). The
Inuit Land Claim and Constitutional Development in the Northwest
Territories: Implications for Local Governance and Industrial Development:
a Research Proposal. Kingston, Ont.: Queen's University.

A proposal to study the potential impact of the Inuit Tapirisat of Canada
(ITC) landclaims on local governance in the ITC area.

3-32   Inuit Claim Management Role in Land and Resources. (1982, August 15).
Nunavut Newsletter, (3), 1-6.

Start of negotiations between Inuit of Nunavut and the Federal Government
of Canada on the Land and Resources proposal, including the Nunavut
Planning Review Board, the Nunavut Lands Authority and the Nunavut
Impact Review Board. List of negotiators and representatives present.

3-33   Inuit Land Claims. (1976, April). Inuit Today, 5(4), 26-33.

Explanation of the concept of Nunavut as presented in the proposal to the
Federal Government by the Inuit Tapirisat of Canada in 1975, including
hunting, fishing, and trapping rights; the Inuit Development Corporation; the
social and economic program; and public lands. (Part 2 of article in "Inuit
Today", 5(3) (March 1976) pages 22-32).

3-34   Inuit Tapirisat of Canada (1980). Address to the 9th Legislative Council of the
Northwest Territories October 1980. Yellowknife, N.W.T.: Inuit Tapirisat
of Canada.

Text of the presentation by ITC (Inuit Tapirisat of Canada) to the territorial
Council on their proposal to create Nunavut and the need for government
consensus in the Northwest Territories.

3-35   Inuit Tapirisat of Canada (1976). Agreement in Principle as to the Settlement of Inuit Land Claims in the Northwest Territories and the Yukon Territory Between the Government of Canada and the Inuit Tapirisat of Canada. Ottawa, Ont.: Inuit Tapirisat of Canada.

   Cover title: "Nunavut: a proposal for the settlement of Inuit lands in the Northwest Territories". A draft Agreement-in-Principle as to the settlement of Inuit landclaims in the N.W.T and the Yukon between the Government of Canada and the Inuit Tapirisat of Canada. Dated February 27, 1976.

3-36   Inuit Tapirisat of Canada. Annual Report. Ottawa, Ont.: Inuit Tapirisat of Canada.

   This report from the major Inuit organization Inuit Tapirisat of Canada (I.T.C.) covers its activities in political, cultural and economic areas, and its regional affiliates in the eastern Arctic and northern Quebec.

3-37   Inuit Tapirisat of Canada (1976). Land Use Database: an Appendix to the Inuit Land Use and Occupancy Project Report, Keewatin. Ottawa, Ont.: Department of Indian Affairs and Northern Development.

   Contains tabulations of land use for each category recognized during field work and for each individual interviewed in the Keewatin District during the Inuit Land Use and Occupancy Project.

3-38   Inuit Tapirisat of Canada (1976). Land Use Database: an Appendix to the Inuit Land Use and Occupancy Project Report, North Baffin. Ottawa, Ont.: Department of Indian Affairs and Northern Development.

   Contains tabulations of land use for each category recognized during field work and for each individual interviewed in the North Baffin area during the Inuit Land Use and Occupancy Project.

3-39   Inuit Tapirisat of Canada (1976). Land Use Database: an Appendix to the Inuit Land Use and Occupancy Project Report, South Baffin. Ottawa, Ont.: Department of Indian Affairs and Northern Development.

   Contains tabulations of land use for each category recognized during field work and for each individual interviewed in the South Baffin area during the Inuit Land Use Occupancy Project.

3-40   Inuit Tapirisat of Canada (1976). Land Use Database: an Appendix to the Inuit Land Use and Occupancy Project report, Western Arctic. Ottawa, Ont.: Department of Indian Affairs and Northern Development.

   Contains tabulations of land use for each category recognized during fieldwork and for each individual interviewed in the Western Arctic. Report includes the Paulatuk, Tuktoyaktuk and Yukon Coast-Delta areas.

3-41   Inuit Tapirisat of Canada (1976). <u>Nunavut: a Proposal for the Settlement of Inuit Lands in the Northwest Territories</u>. s.l.: Inuit Tapirisat of Canada.

Text [not authoritative] of proposed settlement of Inuit landclaims in the eastern Northwest Territories, leading to creation of Nunavut, including summary of basic goals and general statement of policy and intent on the part of the Inuit Tapirisat of Canada.

3-42   Inuit Tapirisat of Canada (1981). <u>Parnagujuk: Basic Objectives of a Comprehensive Blueprint for the North</u>. Ottawa, Ont.: Inuit Tapirisat of Canada.

Presents basic concepts and objectives of Inuit Tapirisat of Canada in their negotiations with the Canadian federal government over land tenure in the north.

3-43   Inuit Tapirisat of Canada (1979). <u>Political Development in Nunavut</u>. Ottawa, Ont.: Information Services, Inuit Tapirisat of Canada.

A report prepared for the Board of Directors of Inuit Tapirisat of Canada, to be discussed at the annual General Meeting, September 3-7, 1979, on the possibilities for political development in Nunavut.

3-44   Inuit Tapirisat of Canada. (1976, March). The Proposal for Inuit Land Claims. <u>Inuit Today</u>, 5(3), 22-32.

Explanation of the proposals presented to the Federal Cabinet in February 1976 for a land sharing agreement between the Inuit and the government of Canada.

3-45   Inuit Tapirisat of Canada (1977). <u>Speaking For the First Citizens of the Canadian Arctic</u>. Ottawa, Ont.: Inuit Tapirisat of Canada.

Explains the Inuit, the Inuit Tapirisat of Canada, and their landclaims. In English and syllabics.

3-46   Inuit Want New Province, Share of Oil, Gas Wealth. (1981). <u>Musk-Ox</u>,(28), 104-105.

Comment on proposed legislation setting rules for northern oil and gas development that could provide sufficient revenue to Inuit to set up a new territory (Nunavut) in the eastern Arctic, including a statement by the Inuit Tapirisat of Canada on aboriginal rights.

3-47   Ipellie, A. (1980, October). Nunavut Leadership Workshop. <u>Inuit Today</u>, (8), 16-30.

Account of a workshop held in Frobisher Bay (Iqaluit) N.W.T. in May 1980, for current and potential leaders of Inuit organizations concerned with the promotion and development of Nunavut.

3-48   Ipellie, A. (1981, November). Nunavut is Here Now and For the Future. Inuit Today, (9), 4-6.

Editorial on the importance of the plebiscite to be held in the Northwest Territories in 1982, on division into Nunavut and a second region.

3-49   ITC and Nunavut Gov't. (1977, March). Inuit Today, 6(3), 51- 52.

Discussion of the future structure and function of ITC (Inuit Tapirisat of Canada) during the General Assembly in Fort Chimo, Quebec, 1977.

3-50   ITC Forms Nunavut Plebiscite Committee. (1982, February 5). News Inuit, 1-2.

Announcement that the Inuit Tapirisat of Canada (ITC) has formed its own committee to inform northern residents of the plebiscite on division of the N.W.T. (to be held April 14, 1982) following the Federal government refusal of funding for a committee.

3-51   Jull, P. (1982, September). Next Steps For Nunavut. Policy Options Politiques, 3(5), 6-10.

Assessment of the state of negotiations on Nunavut following the plebiscite in April 1982 on division of the N.W.T.

3-52   Jull, P. (1982). Nunavut. Northern Perspectives, 10(2), 1-8.

Discussion of proposal to create a new territory in eastern part of Northwest Territories, to be put to plebiscite in April 1982.

3-53   Land Claims Negotiations 1982 Annual Report. (1983, April). Nunavut Newsletter, 10-12.

Report on landclaims negotiations for Nunavut in 1982, including the NLA (Nunavut Lands Authority), Inuit lands, municipal lands, land use planning, the question of political settlement and the mandate of the federal Chief Negotiator.

3-54   Landmark Decision. (1982, December). Nunavut Newsletter, (6), 2.

Announcement of apparent change in the position of the Federal Government of Canada on division of the Northwest Territories, i.e. formation of Nunavut before settlement of landclaims, or linking of political and landclaim questions.

3-55   Lester, G. S. (1982, June 15). Guest Editorial by Geoff Lester, Former Researcher and Member of the Negotiation Team of the Nunavut Land Claims Project. Nunavut Newsletter, (1), 6-7.

Commentary on the position of the Office of Native Claims on the Nunavut Wildlife Agreement-in-Principle.

3-56   Lester, G. S. (1981). The Territorial Rights of the Inuit of the Canadian
         Northwest Territories: A Legal Argument. Doctoral Dissertation, York
         University, Toronto, Ont.

         Examines the issue of aboriginal landclaims by Inuit of the N.W.T.

3-57   Mahoney [Justice]. (1980). The Baker Lake Decision on Aboriginal Rights.
         Musk-Ox, (26), 59-77.

         Discussion of the rationale for, and implications of, the court finding that
         aboriginal title exists in the Baker Lake area of the Northwest Territories.
         Residents were concerned that the caribou herds would be affected by
         mining activities proposed by Cominco Lt. and Pan Ocean Oil Ltd. Includes
         text of the judgment and maps of the relevant areas, and a comparison with
         the Calder Case in British Columbia.

3-58   The Main Features of the Nunavut Land and Resources Position. (1982, July
         15). Nunavut Newsletter, (2), 2-3.

         Name change of Nunavut Governing Body (NGB) to Tungavik Federation
         of Nunavut (TFN), with objectives and membership.

3-59   McConnell, W. H. (1973). The Calder Case in Historical Perspective.
         Saskatchewan Law Review, 38, 88-122.

         Discussion of the landmark Calder case (1973) in which the Nishga Indians
         of British Columbia who have never signed any treaties with the central
         government, asked the Supreme Court of Canada to recognize their
         aboriginal title to their lands.

3-60   McConnell, W. H., & Milligan, S. M. (1981, December). The "Drury Report" on
         Constitutional Development in the Northwest Territories. Musk-ox, (29),
         10-24.

         Discussion of the Drury Report on whether the Northwest Territories
         should be divided or otherwise organized.

3-61   Merritt, J. (1980, February). Nunavut Negotiations Delayed. ITC News, 5.

         Account of delays in the landclaims negotiation process for Nunavut
         resulting from a Federal election and the necessity for a new mandate for the
         Department of Indian Affairs and Northern Development (DIAND) to be
         decided by the Federal Cabinet.

3-62   Milton Freeman Research Ltd. (1976). Inuit Land Use and Occupancy Project:
         a Report. Ottawa, Ont.: Dept. of Indian Affairs and Northern Development.

         Vol. 1: Land use and occupancy. Vol. 2: Supporting studies. Vol. 3:
         Land use atlas. A comprehensive and verifiable record of Inuit land use and
         occupancy in the Canadian north. Vol. 2 includes details of a data base
         produced from the information collected for the project (p. 61-67).

3-63   Negotiations to Start on Land and Resources in Nunavut. (1982, July 15).
       Nunavut Newsletter, (2), 1.

       Announcement at start of negotiations on land and resources in Nunavut,
       calling for a joint-management approach.

3-64   New Administration Policy for Land Claims. (1982, October). Nunavut
       Newsletter, (5), 11-12.

       Change in administration policy for funding of the Nunavut Land Claims
       Project by the Tungavik Federation of Nunavut.

3-65   Nunavut - A Comprehensive Claim. (1976). Musk-Ox, (18), 3- 41.

       Summary of the Federal policy on comprehensive claims in the mid 1970's,
       text of the Nunavut Proposal, with commentary and map, memorandum by
       Dr. Norman Ward, followed by debates of the N.W.T. Council of May 26
       and May 28, 1976 when the Nunavut Proposal was being discussed.

3-66   Nunavut: A New Government for the North: A New Partner in Confederation
       = Nunavut: un Nouveau Governement pour le Nord: un Nouveau
       Partenaire dans la Confederation. (n.d.). : N.W.T. Department of
       Information.

       Pamphlet which describes Nunavut, a proposal for territorial-type
       government to be established by Inuit beyond treeline in N.W.T. Also
       discusses steps in development of native self-government. Text in English,
       French and the native language.

3-67   The Nunavut Concept: A Proposal For Inuit Self-Determination. (1981,
       December). Arjungnagimmat, 19-54.

       Discussion of the special session of the Territorial Council in Frobisher Bay
       (Iqaluit) in 1981, to consider the concept of Nunavut and its implications for
       northern residents.

3-68   Nunavut Constitutional Forum. (1985, October 15). Northern Decisions, 3(12),
       90.

       Report of four resolutions passed at the meeting of the Nunavut
       Constitutional Forum in Coppermine, September 25-27, 1985.

3-69   Nunavut Governing Body. (1982, June 15). Nunavut Newsletter, (1), 3.

       Announcement of the formation of the Nunavut Governing Body (NGB) as
       the aim of ITC (Inuit Tapirisat of Canada) which will have responsibility for
       landclaims and political development in the N.W.T.

3-70   Nunavut Inuit Tapirisat's Proposal to Split the NWT. (1980, January). Inuit
        North, 1-7.

        Outlines the Inuit Tapirisat's Proposal for the establishment of Nunavut and
        various reactions to it.

3-71   Nunavut Lands Authority. (1982, October). Nunavut Newsletter, (5), 2-3.

        Progress of negotiations on the Land and Resources Agreement, based on a
        comprehensive approach to ownership and management of all lands in
        Nunavut, including the role of the Nunavut Lands Authority (NLA) and the
        Nunavut Impact Review Board (NIRB), and outline of the proposed
        economic benefits of the Agreement.

3-72   Nunavut Newsletter. (1982). Ottawa, Ont.: Nunavut Land Claims Project,
        Tungavik Federation of Nunavut.

        Periodical publication providing information on the political activity of
        native peoples towards the establishment of the proposed Nunavut region.
        The issues dealt with revolve around the central theme of self-determination
        through political process: devolution, constitutional development, division,
        landclaims, natural and environmental policy, historical resource law, and
        social and economic policy. (Name changed to Nunavut, with v.3 no. 8,
        1984).

3-73   Nunavut Our Land. (1976, March). C.A.S.N.P. Bulletin, (19), 19-20.

        Summary of the rationale for an Inuit landclaim as defined by the Inuit
        Tapirisat of Canada (ITC) and the eventual creation of Nunavut.

3-74   Nunavut Plebiscite. (n.d.). Ottawa, Ont.: Inuit Tapirisat of Canada.

        Press kit containing background information about the Nunavut concept of
        dividing the existing Northwest Territories from 1975 up to April 14, 1982
        when the people of the Territories will vote on a plebiscite regarding
        division. Includes chronology of events, maps of proposed boundaries and
        the plebiscite ordinance.

3-75   Nunavut: Summary of a Working Paper on the Nunavut Proposal. (1976).
        Ottawa, Ont.: s.n.

        Notes on paper prepared by Northern Program DINA, and Northern
        Administration, N.W.T. Government (June 17, 1976).

3-76   N.W.T. Inuit Land Claims Commission (1978). Inuit Nunangat, the People's
        Land: A Struggle for Survival. Frobisher Bay: The Commission.

        Includes Proposed Agreement-in-Principle for the establishment of Inuit
        rights between the Inuit and the Government of Canada.

3-77   N.W.T. Working Towards Nunavut. (1982, December). <u>Nunavut Newsletter,</u>
        (6), 3-6.

        Discussion of the work of the Tungavik Federation of Nunavut and the
        Constitutional Alliance of the Northwest Territories (Western Constitutional
        Forum or WCF and Nunavut Constitutional Forum or NCF), as well as the
        positions of the Federal Government of Canada and the Government of the
        Northwest Territories on land use and social impact assessments.

3-78   <u>Outpost Camp Data, Northwest Territories, 1977-1985.</u> (1985). Yellowknife,
        N.W.T.: Government of the Northwest Territories.

        Detailed statistics of numbers, location, and cost of outpost camps in the
        Northwest Territories, compiled for 1977-1985 from applications for
        financial assistance made to the territorial government, with a discussion of
        the "Back To Land Program" and its significance in landclaim negotiations
        such as Nunavut.

3-79   Pact With Inuit Nears Draft Stage. (1981). <u>Musk-Ox,</u> (28), 105-106.

        Report of the talks on wildlife and harvesting issues between federal
        government officials and the Inuit Tapirisat of Canada, as a preliminary to
        achieving political control of the eastern part of the Northwest Territories
        (Nunavut).

3-80   Paulette, F. (1973). <u>In the Matter of: an Application by Chief Francois Paulette
        et al., to Lodge a Certain Caveat With the Registrar of Titles of the Land
        Titles Office for the Northwest Territories.</u> s.l.: s.n.

        Transcripts of the proceedings, judgment, and reasons for judgment
        regarding a caveat filed to protect an interest in 400,000 square miles of
        land of the N.W.T and based on a claim for aboriginal rights.

3-81   Penner, K. (1978). <u>Dene and Metis Claims in the Mackenzie Valley: Proposals
        For Discussion, Yellowknife, N.W.T., January 24, 1978.</u> Ottawa, Ont.:
        Indian and Northern Affairs.

        Proposals put forward to the Metis Association of the Northwest
        Territories and to the Indian Brotherhood of the Northwest Territories by
        the federal government representative on native landclaims.

3-82   Political Development in Nunavut. (1979, November). <u>ITC News,</u> 1-2.

        Discussion of the document "Political Development in Nunavut", containing
        the proposals for an Inuit territory.

3-83   <u>Political Development in Nunavut: an Analysis Prepared by the Dept. of Local
        Government, Baffin Region.</u> (1980). Iqaluit, N.W.T.: Dept. of Local
        Government.

        Discussion of the relationship of landclaims and political matters in the
        proposed new territory of Nunavut.

3-84   Political Development in Nunavut. (1980, January). The Inuit North, 45-55.

This document was presented to the September 1979 meeting, in Igloolik, Northwest Territories, of Inuit Tapirisat of Canada (ITC). It outlines present political development, the need for Nunavut, human rights, jurisdiction (provincial, regional, or other), landclaims, land and resources, financial aspects, and the long term outlook.

3-85   Political Development in Nunavut. (1980, December). Inuit Today, (8), 78-96.

Text of the document prepared for the Board of Directors of the Inuit Tapirisat of Canada for the July 1980 annual meeting in Coppermine, N.W.T., dealing with political developments in the North; the need for Nunavut; the Use and Occupancy Project; human rights; jurisdiction; and the federal role.

3-86   Proposed Agreement-in-Principle for the Establishment of Inuit Rights Between the Inuit of Nunavut and the Government of Canada. (1977). s.l.: s.n.

Draft for discussion drawn up by the Nunavut Land Claims Commission at meetings in Rankin Inlet and Cambridge Bay, June 1977.

3-87   Regional Governments for Nunavut. (1982, February). Nunavut Newsletter, 3.

Resolution by the NCF (Nunavut Constitutional Forum) to provide for regional governments in the future territory.

3-88   Report of the Advisory Commission on the Development of Government in the Northwest Territories. (1966). Ottawa, Ont.: Dept. of Indian Affairs and Northern Development.

Report on matters related to the political development of the N.W.T., organized under six major subjects: evolution of the present form of government in the N.W.T.; functional review of government in the N.W.T. today (by individual department); non-governmental problems of the north that relate to forms of government; alternative programs for political development; postulates; recommendations. Known as the Carrothers Commission or Carrothers Report.

3-89   Settlement of Land Claims Gaining Momentum Before Federal Election. (1984, April). Nunasi Report, 1(2), 10-11.

Account of various viewpoints on extinguishment of aboriginal rights in the Nunavut and Denendeh landclaims area.

3-90   Seventeen Topics Have Been Successfully Negotiated. (1986, October). Nunavut, 5(10), 7.

Summary chart of seventeen topics negotiated to date to the stage of Agreement-in-Principle, by the Tungavik Federation of Nunavut and the Federal Government of Canada.

3-91   Significant Events on the Road to Nunavut. (1992, March). Nunavut, 11(2), 36-40.

Chronology of major turning points in the history of the concept of Nunavut and Denendeh from 1926 to 1999.

3-92   Slattery, B. (1979). The Land Rights of Indigenous Canadian Peoples, as Affected by the Crown's Acquisition of Their Territories. Doctoral Thesis, University of Saskatchewan, Native Law Centre, Saskatoon, Sask.

The problem examined in this work is whether the land rights originally held by Canada's indigenous peoples survived the process whereby the British Crown acquired sovereignty over their territories, and, if so, in what form.

3-93   Summary Comparison of the Government "White Paper" and the Indians "Red Paper". (1970). Winterburn, Alta.: Indian Association of Alberta.

Comparison in table form of the assumptions and provisions of the Government of Canada's 1969 "White Paper" on status and treatment of native peoples, and the Indian Association of Alberta's 1970 "Red Paper" responding to it.

3-94   Tagak Curley. (1982, July 15). Nunavut Newsletter, (2), 5.

Appointment of the president of the Nunasi Development Corporation to the board of directors of Borealis Exploration Limited which proposed an open-pit, iron ore mine in Melville Peninsula.

3-95   Tester, F. J. (1980). And the First Shall be Last: Some Social Implications of the Baker Lake Decision. Northern Perspectives, 8(3), 9-12.

Review of the law case establishing landclaims and aboriginal rights of Baker Lake Eskimos, 1979.

3-96   Trudeau, P. (1970). Statement by the Prime Minister at a Meeting With the Indian Association of Alberta and the National Indian Brotherhood, Ottawa, June 4, 1970. s.l.: s.n.

General discussion about problem of Canadian Indian rights. Examines federal government's "White Paper" proposals and Indian "Red Paper" proposals and emphasizes difficulty of bringing about a mutually acceptable solution.

3-97   Tungavik Federation to Negotiate Nunavut Claim. (1982, October). Project North Newsletter, 6(4), 6-7.

Announcement of the incorporation of the Nunavut governing body as the Tungavik Federation of Nunavut, to take over responsibility for Nunavut landclaims from the Inuit Tapirisat of Canada.

3-98   Union of British Columbia Indian Chiefs (1971). Aboriginal Title and Rights
        Position Paper: Our Land is Our Future: Ratified at the UBIC 17th Annual
        General Assembly. Vancouver, B.C.: The Union.

        Statement of position on landclaims and rights by the First Nations of
        British Columbia, including self-determination, inherent sovereignty,
        decolonization and Canada's conditional sovereignty.

3-99   Update on Nunavut. (1982, September 15). Nunavut Newsletter, (4), 1-2.

        Update on progress of negotiations on land and resources, and on funding
        from the Federal Government.

3-100   Usher, P. J. (1973). The Committee for Original Peoples' Entitlement. Inuvik,
        N.W.T.: Committee for Original Peoples' Entitlement.

        The history and policies of COPE, an organization of Northwest Territories
        native peoples.

3-101   Usher, P. J., & Beakhust, G. (1973). Land Regulation in the Canadian North.
        Ottawa, Ont.: Canadian Arctic Resources Committee.

        An analysis of the problem of competition for land use in northern
        development and an evaluation of the function and effect of the present
        regulations.

3-102   Ward, N. W. (1976). Report Prepared for the Council of the N.W.T. on the
        Proposal Entitled "Nunavut" Made by the Inuit Tapirisat of Canada to the
        Government of Canada, February 1976. Yellowknife, N.W.T.: Council for
        the Northwest Territories.

        Critical analysis of the proposal for formation of the territory of Nunavut,
        with discussion of basic terms and definitions.

3-103   Weaver, S. M. (1981). Making Canadian Indian Policy: The Hidden Agenda
        1968-70. Toronto, Ont.: University of Toronto Press.

        An analysis of the formulation of the Canadian government's White Paper
        on Indian policy based on interviews with individuals involved in shaping the
        policy, government documents and reports, and published materials.

3-104   Working Paper: Report of the Honourable C.M. Drury, Special Representative
        to the Prime Minister for Constitutional Development in the Northwest
        Territories. (1979). Yellowknife, N.W.T.: Office of the Special
        Representative for Constitutional Development in the Northwest Territories.

        Set of 8 working papers on constitutional development in the N.W.T.
        Includes native peoples in the N.W.T.: status and claims; N.W.T.
        comprehensive claims; assessment of Inuvialuit Land Rights Agreement-in-
        Principle; rights and politics in the Canadian setting; Government of the
        Northwest Territories; community government and regionalism in the
        N.W.T.; land and resources; and other federal responsibilities in the N.W.T.

3-105   Yukon Native Brotherhood (1973). Together Today for Our Children
        Tomorrow: A Statement of Grievances and an Approach to Settlement by
        the Yukon Indian People. Whitehorse, Yukon: Council for Yukon Indians.

        Report prepared by the Yukon Native Brotherhood for the Commissioner
        on Indian claims and the Government of Canada relating the concerns and
        grievances of the Yukon Indian people.

SECTION 4: HISTORICAL 1983-1993

4-1   The 1987 Constitutional Accord. (1988). Yellowknife, N.W.T.: Government of
        the N.W.T.

        A statement of position by the Minister of Justice for the Northwest
        Territories on the effect of the proposed Meech Lake Constitutional Accord
        on the Territories.

4-2   Achieving a Final Agreement. (1991, July). Nunavut, 10(2), 4-6.

        Summary of tasks to be completed between signing of the Nunavut
        Agreement-in-Principle in Igloolik, April 1990, and the anticipated Final
        Agreement and ratification.

4-3   Agreement Between the Inuit of the Nunavut Settlement Area and Her Majesty
        in Right of Canada: Official Version for the Inuit Ratification Vote. (1992).
        Yellowknife, N.W.T.: Inuit Ratification Committee.

        Authoritative text of the Agreement between the Inuit of the Nunavut
        Settlement Area (eastern part of the Northwest Territories) and the
        Government of Canada, prepared for a ratification vote by the Inuit as
        represented by the Tungavik Federation of Nunavut (TFN). Includes legal
        description of boundaries and map (for information only). Terms cover
        political development, wildlife, compensation, outpost camps, land and
        resource management and planning, water rights, marine areas, landfast ice
        zone, land title and access, taxation, government employment and contracts,
        resource royalties, the Nunavut Trust, the Nunavut Social Development
        Council, archaeology, enrollment and ratification process, implementation
        and arbitration.

4-4   Agreement Between the Inuit of the Nunavut Settlement Area and Her Majesty
        the Queen in Right of Canada. (1993). Ottawa, Ont.: Joint Authority of the
        Tungavik and the Honourable Tom Siddon, P.C., M.P., Minister of Indian
        Affairs and Northern Development.

        Text of the Agreement between the Inuit of the Nunavut Settlement Area
        [eastern part of the Northwest Territories] and the Government of Canada,
        as signed by representatives of the Tungavik Federation of Nunavut (TFN)
        and the Federal Government in Iqaluit May 25, 1993. Includes legal
        description of boundaries and map (for information only). Terms cover
        political development, wildlife, compensation, outpost camps, parks, land

and resource management and planning, water rights, marine areas, landfast ice zone, municipal lands, land title and access, taxation, government employment and contracts, resource royalties, capital transfer, Inuit Impact and Benefit Agreements (IIBAs), the Inuit Heritage Trust, the Nunavut Trust, the Nunavut Social Development Council, archaeology, enrollment and ratification process, implementation and arbitration, relations with Inuit of northern Quebec, other aboriginal peoples in the Territories and the Denesuline of northern Manitoba and Saskatchewan.

4-5   Agreement for Division of the N.W.T. (1987). s.l.: s.n.

Several communications regarding an agreement on a boundary for the division of the N.W.T. Includes: 1) Memorandum of understanding between the Nunavut Constitutional Forum and the Western Constitutional Forum concerning recommendations to the Legislative Assembly. 2) News release Boundary agreement reached. 3) Official summary of the boundary and constitutional agreement. 4) Boundary and constitutional agreement for the implementation of division of the N.W.T between the Western Constitutional Forum and the Nunavut Constitutional Forum.

4-6   Agreements Recognize Economic Value of Inuit Land Title. (1983, May). Nunavut Newsletter, 3-5.

Details of agreements on guidelines for Inuit land identification and on outpost camps.

4-7   Alliance Meets But Still No Agreement on a Boundary to Divide the NWT. (1986, August). Building Blocks, (4), 1.

Meeting of the Constitutional Alliance of the Northwest Territories to discuss the boundary issue on division of the Territories.

4-8   Allooloo, T. (1990). Article 4 TFN Agreement-in-Principle. Yellowknife, N.W.T.: Government of the Northwest Territories.

This statement by the Associate Minister, Aboriginal Rights and Constitutional Development, Northwest Territories, describes the agreement between the Governments of Canada and the Northwest Territories and the Tungavik Federation of Nunavut, on the establishment of Nunavut as a primary subdivision of the Northwest Territories, and on the delineation of a boundary.

4-9   Allooloo, T. (1991). TFN Boundary Agreement: and Related Correspondence. Yellowknife, N.W.T.: Government of the Northwest Territories.

Announcement by Titus Allooloo, Associate Minister of Aboriginal Rights and Constitutional Development, Northwest Territories, of the agreement between the Tungavik Federation of Nunavut (TFN) and the Government of Canada, on a boundary to divide the Territories into Nunavut (Inuit) and Denendeh (Dene), in settlement of landclaims. Includes correspondence relating to the issue between TFN, the Dene Nation and the (federal) Minister of Indian Affairs and Northern Development.

4-10   Amagoalik, J. (1992, May). The 4th of May. Nunavut, 11(3), 12.

        Commentary on the significance of the plebiscite of May 4, 1992 on the proposed boundary between Nunavut and the rest of the Northwest Territories.

4-11   Amagoalik, J. (1992, January). The Land Claim and Nunavut: One Without the Other Isn't Enough. Arctic Circle, 2(4), 20.

        Explanation of the importance of the link between landclaim settlements and the creation of Nunavut.

4-12   Amagoalik, J. (1986, November). Nunavut is Focus of Shared Identity. Nunavut, 5(11), 10.

        Rebuttal by the chairman of the Nunavut Constitutional Forum, of an article putting the case against division of the Northwest Territories into Nunavut and the western territories.

4-13   Amagoalik, J. (1987, March). The Way is Open to Create Nunavut. Nunavut, 6(3), 2-6.

        Special edition of Nunavut with detailed summary of the Iqaluit Agreement, an agreement between the leaders of the Western Constitutional Forum (WCF) and the Nunavut Constitutional Forum (NCF) on the proposed boundary and the terms, conditions and schedules for division of Nunavut and Denendeh of the N.W.T. Includes map, summary of the principles to guide the creation of Nunavut, details of NCF and WCF and Inuvialiut regional government.

4-14   Ames, R. (1992, May). Land Claim Ratification Tours. Nunavut, 11(3), 4.

        Details of who can vote, where and when, in the Nov. 3-5, 1992 Ratification Vote on the Nunavut Land Agreement.

4-15   Ames, R., Axford, D., Usher, P. J., Weick, E., & Wenzel, G. (1989). Keeping on the Land: a Study of the Feasibility of a Comprehensive Wildlife Harvest Support Programme in the Northwest Territories. Ottawa, Ont.: Canadian Arctic Resources Committee.

        Assesses the viability of a wildlife harvest support program through an examination of the socio-economic aspects of hunting, the design and implementation of a support program and the issues and problems surrounding its application to northern hunters.

4-16   Annual General Meeting Looks at Board Structure. (1986, November). Nunavut, 5(11), 8.

        Summary of resolutions passed at the annual general meeting of the Tungavik Federation of Nunavut, October 1986, including changes to board membership and structure.

4-17   Annual Meeting. (1983, March). <u>Nunavut Newsletter</u>, 6-8.

Annual report of the activities of the Tungavik Federation of Nunavut and of the Nunavut Land Claims Project for 1982-1983.

4-18   Archaeology Provisions for an Agreement-in-Principle Signed July 23. (1983, August). <u>Nunavut Newsletter</u>, 5-8.

Provisions of the archaeology agreement-in-principle, signed July 23, 1983, giving Inuit of Nunavut greater control and responsibility over archaeological activities and artifacts, and establishing the Inuit Heritage Trust.

4-19   Artifacts Tell Stories About the Past. (1987, October). <u>Nunavut</u>, 6(8), 8.

Note on the agreement between the Tungavik Federation of Nunavut and the Federal Government of Canada on control and management of archaeological sites and artifacts.

4-20   Assembly Reviews Paper on Claims, Division, Devolution. (1986, July). <u>Building Blocks</u>, (3), 3.

Discussion in the Legislative Assembly of the Northwest Territories landclaims, division of the Territories, and devolution of powers from federal to territorial level.

4-21   <u>Background Materials Regarding the Plebiscite on the Division Boundary to be Held on May 4 1992</u>. (1992). Yellowknife, N.W.T.: Government of the Northwest Territories.

Collection of materials to serve as an aid in interpreting the history of the vote on the boundary between the proposed territories of Nunavut and Denendeh. Includes a chronology of significant events, the Iqaluit Agreement, Parker Report, Legislative Assembly discussions, summary of the Nunavut Land Claim Agreement, and text of the Plebiscite Proclamation.

4-22   Baffled by NIRB, SEARP, EARP and FEARO? (1983, January). <u>Nunavut Newsletter</u>, 4-5.

Explanation of SEARP (Socio-economic Environmental Assessment Review Panel), NIRB (Nunavut Impact Review Board), FEARO (Federal Environmental Assessment Review Office) and EARP (Environmental Assessment Review Process).

4-23   Bankes, N. (1987). The Place of Land-Use Planning in the TFN Claim. In T. Fenge, & W. Rees (Editors), <u>Hinterland or Homeland? Land Use Planning in Northern Canada</u>. , (pp. 95-112). Ottawa, Ont.: Canadian Arctic Resources Committee.

Outline of the position on land-use planning that has been taken by TFN (Tungavik Federation of Nunavut) in its claim negotiations with the Federal Government of Canada, in the context of TFN's overall position on land and resources.

4-24   Bankes, N. (1987, October). The Status of Hudson Bay. <u>Northern Perspectives</u>, 15(3), 14-15.

       Discussion of the legal status of islands and offshore areas of the Hudson Bay (federal, provincial, territorial or within new jurisdictions such as Nunavut) and of the laws applicable to hunting in the area, and of claims of unextinguished aboriginal title.

4-25   Bell, J. (1992, January). Nunavut: The Quiet Revolution. <u>Arctic Circle</u>, 2(4), 12-21.

       Analysis of progress to date in negotiations between the Inuit of Nunavut and the Federal Government of Canada on landclaims, political control, and economic development.

4-26   Bell, J. (1991, September). A Time for Candour. <u>Arctic Circle</u>, 2(2), 11-12.

       Commentary on political attitudes in the Northwest Territories, including the territorial system of consensus and the creation of Nunavut.

4-27   The Boundary. (1992, March). <u>Nunavut</u>, 11(2), 9-10.

       Summary of the history of the proposed boundary between Nunavut and the rest of the Northwest Territories to be voted on in the plebiscite of May 4, 1992.

4-28   Boundary Agreement Passes 1st Hurdle Then Stumbles: Plebiscite Postponed. (1987, June). <u>Building Blocks</u>, (7), 1.

       Article on the delay in a plebiscite on the division of the Northwest Territories because of disagreement on boundary overlap areas.

4-29   <u>Boundary and Constitutional Agreement for the Implementation of Division of the Northwest Territories Between the Western Constitutional Forum and the Nunavut Constitutional Forum, January 15, 1987, Iqaluit, Nunavut.</u> (1987). Ottawa, Ont.: Canadian Arctic Resources Committee in Cooperation With the Nunavut Constitutional Forum and Western Constitutional Forum.

       Text of agreement on issues required to implement division of the Northwest Territories dated January 15, 1987.

4-30   [Boundary Discussions]. (1985, September 27). <u>News Release (Western Constitutional Forum)</u>, 1-4.

       Commentary on decision by the Nunavut Constitutional Forum to withdraw from the Constitutional Alliance of the Northwest Territories (at the Coppermine Constitutional Conference), with chronology of progress on division and boundary selection.

4-31   Boundary Lines are Needed for Both Claims and Division. (1987, April).
        Nunavut, 6(4), 2-4.

        Discussion of the announcement by the Dene/Metis Negotiating Secretariat
        that they were withdrawing support of the May 1984 Overlap Agreement
        with the Inuvialiut, and the boundary lines of Nunavut, Denendeh and the
        Inuvialiut Settlement Region.

4-32   Breakdown in Negotiations. (1983, February). Nunavut Newsletter, 2.

        Suspension of negotiations on the landclaim by the Tungavik Federation of
        Nunavut, after the decision of the Federal Government of Canada to restrict
        Inuit to advisory roles in the settlement in relation to NIRB (Nunavut
        Impact Review Board), disallowance, the inquiries act and the question of
        arbitration.

4-33   BRIA and ITC Election Results. (1983, May). Nunavut Newsletter, 10.

        Election results for the boards of BRIA (Baffin Region Inuit Association)
        and TFN (Tungavik Federation of Nunavut).

4-34   Briefing Kit on Devolution and Related Issues Prepared for the Nunavut
        Constitutional Forum. (1986, May). Ottawa, Ont.: Inuit Committee on
        National Issues.

        Collection of correspondence and minutes of meetings between Inuit,
        Dene/Metis and the Federal Government groups, and of the Nunavut
        Working Group, concerning their positions on devolution and proposals for
        a Memorandum of Understanding (MOU). Documents assembled by the
        Inuit Committee on National Issues (I.C.N.I.).

4-35   Building Nunavut: a Working Document With a Proposal for an Arctic
        Constitution = Batir Le Nunavut: un Document de Travail Accompagne de
        Propositions En Vue D'une Constitution de L'Arctique. (1983).
        Yellowknife, N.W.T.: Nunavut Constitutional Forum.

        Outlines the aims behind establishing Nunavut and contains proposals for a
        constitution for a Nunavut government.

4-36   Canada. Indian and Northern Affairs Canada (1990). Agreement-in-Principle
        Between the Inuit of the Nunavut Settlement Area and Her Majesty
        in Right of Canada. Ottawa, Ont.: Joint Authority of the Tungavik
        Federation of Nunavut and the Minister of Indian Affairs and
        Northern Development.

        Text of the agreement between the native peoples of the Nunavut region of
        the Northwest Territories (eastern Arctic and the mainland north of the
        treeline), as represented by the Tungavik Federation of Nunavut, and the
        Federal Government, in order to define landclaims.

4-37   Canada. Parliament. House of Commons (34th, 3rd Session: 1993) (1993). Bill C-132, Statutes of Canada, Chapter 28: an Act to Establish a Territory to be Known as Nunavut and Provide for its Government and to Amend Certain Acts in Consequence Thereof = Project de Loi C-132, Lois du Canada, 1993, Chapitre 28: loi Concernant la Creation du Territoire du Nunavut et L'Organisation de son Gouvernement, et Modifiant Diverses Lois en Consequence. Ottawa, Ont.: Queen's Printer.

        Text of the legislation (Nunavut Act) establishing the territory of Nunavut (eastern Northwest Territories) and its form and method of government.

4-38   Canada. Parliament. House of Commons (1993). Bill C-133: An Act Respecting an Agreement Between the Inuit of the Nunavut Settlement Area and Her Majesty the Queen in Right of Canada. First Reading May 28, 1993. Ottawa, Ont.: Minister of Indian Affairs and Northern Development.

        Text of the Nunavut Land Claims Agreement Act (Bill C-133) as presented for first reading May 28, 1993, and ratifying the Nunavut Land Claims Agreement.

4-39   Canada. Parliament. House of Commons. Standing Committee on Aboriginal Affairs (1993). Minutes of Proceedings and Evidence of the Standing Committee on Aboriginal Affairs: Respecting, Public Meeting Pursuant to Standing Order 108(2), Study of Overlapping Claims of the Tungavik Federation of Nunavut Boundaries. Ottawa, Ont.: Queen's Printer.

        Transcript of the proceedings of the Standing Committee on Aboriginal Affairs concerning claims by the Tungavik Federation of Nunavut (TFN), the Prince Albert Tribal Council and the Manitoba Keewatin Okimakanak Inc., to overlapping areas of the southern Keewatin, within the proposed boundaries of Nunavut.

4-40   Canada. Parliament. House of Commons. Standing Committee on Aboriginal Affairs. (1993). Minutes of Proceedings and Evidence of the Standing Committee on Aboriginal Affairs: Respecting Pursuant to Standing Order 108(2), Consideration of Overlapping Claims in the Tungavik Federation of Nunavut Boundaries. Ottawa, Ont.: Queen's Printer.

        Transcript of the proceedings of the Standing Committee on Aboriginal Affairs concerning claims by the Tungavik Federation of Nunavut (TFN) and the Denesuline of northern Manitoba to use of areas of the southern Keewatin within the proposed boundaries of Nunavut.

4-41   Canada's Arctic Oasis Will Become Wildlife Area. (1986, September). Nunavut, 5(9), 2.

        Announcement of the designation of Polar Bear Pass on Bathurst Island as northern Canada's first national wildlife area, and its relation to Inuit hunting activities in the region.

4-42   Cherkasov, A. I. (1993, January). Nunavut: The Canadian Experiment in
        Territorial Self-Determination For the Inuit. Polar Geography and Geology,
        17(1), 64-71.

        This article summarizes the negotiations that have led up to the
        achievement of Nunavut and suggests that Russian authorities should be
        preparing to collaborate with the new government of Nunavut on matters of
        common interest, rather than with the governments of Canada or of the
        Northwest Territories as at present.

4-43   Coates, K. S., & Powell, J. (1989). Fighting For Control: Native Politics and
        Land Claims. In K. Coates, & J. Powell, The Modern North: People,
        Politics and the Rejection of Colonialism. , (pp. 100-130). Toronto, Ont.:
        James Lorimer & Company.

        Summary of the growth of native peoples' organizations and the course of
        landclaims negotiations in the North, from 1960's to late 1980's, including
        Nunavut.

4-44   Coleman, G. (1993, March). The Inherited Dream: Looking for Nunavut's Lost
        Generation. Arctic Circle, 14-19, 34-35.

        Discussion of whether younger people and school students will benefit from
        the creation of Nunavut.

4-45   Community Liaison Worker Training Program: A Model for "Pre-Settlement
        Training". (1986). Ottawa, Ont.: Tungavik Federation of Nunavut and the
        Confederation College of Applied Arts and Technology.

        Details of a proposed training program for Inuit community liaison workers
        to qualify them to handle the responsibilities of implementing the Nunavut
        settlement terms of self-government and new decision-making structures.

4-46   Community-Based Observations on Sustainable Development in Southern
        Hudson Bay. (1991, August). Nunavut, 10(3), 14-18.

        Discussion by residents of Sanikiluaq, Belcher Islands, (Hudson Bay) on the
        transboundary effects of hydroelectric power development in Ontario and
        Quebec, on the economy of a Nunavut community.

4-47   Comprehensive Claims Coalition Gets Money From GNWT. (1986, September).
        Building Blocks, (5), 1.

        Summary of activities of the Comprehensive Claims Coalition (including
        TFN), created to lobby for implementation of the Coolican Report, and of
        grants received from the Government of the Northwest Territories to
        support their work.

4-48   Conservation Areas Provisions of an Agreement-in-Principle. (1983). Ottawa,
        Ont.: s.n.

        Draft of sections of the Nunavut Agreement affecting various areas and
        sites defined as conservation areas, and Inuit rights in such areas.

4-49   Constitutional Alliance of the Northwest Territories (1984). Chronological Notes
        on the Western Constitutional Forum of the Constitutional Alliance of the
        Northwest Territories. Yellowknife, N.W.T.: Constitutional Alliance of the
        Northwest Territories.

        Chronological summary of meetings of the Western Constitutional Forum of
        the Constitutional Alliance of the Northwest Territories for the year. The
        principle objective for the Alliance is division of the Territories.

4-50   The Constitutional Alliance of the N.W.T. and the Nunavut and Western
        Constitutional Forums: Report to the Legislative Assembly, March 4, 1983.
        (1983). Yellowknife, N.W.T.: Government of the Northwest Territories.

        This report outlines the mandate of the two Constitutional Forums of the
        Northwest Territories; to identify a suitable boundary for division (into
        Denendeh and Nunavut) and submit it to a forum of public ratification, and
        negotiate the outcome with the Federal Government of Canada.

4-51   Constitutional Alliance Awaits Inuvialuit Opinion. (1985, November 26).
        Western Constitutional Forum Newsletter, (14), 1.

        Account of the meeting of the Western and Nunavut Constitutional Forums
        at Yellowknife, November 3-4, as the Constitutional Alliance of the
        Northwest Territories, for discussion of the boundary question.

4-52   Constitutional Alliance Meets But No Boundary Agreement Yet. (1986,
        September 24). Western Constitutional Forum Newsletter, (19), 1.

        Account of meeting in Winnipeg, August 25-26, 1986 of the Western and
        Nunavut Constitutional Forums, as the Constitutional Alliance of the
        Northwest Territories, at which COPE (Committee For Original Peoples'
        Entitlement) was asked to explore the question of the inclusion of Inuvialuit
        in a western territory.

4-53   Constitutional Alliance of the Northwest Territories. (1987, January 31).
        Northern Decisions, 4(18), 131-132.

        Announcement of the signing of a boundary and constitutional agreement
        (the Iqaluit Agreement) between the Western Constitutional Forum and the
        Nunavut Constitutional Forum, on 15 January, 1987, at Iqaluit, Northwest
        Territories, laying out the terms, conditions, and schedule for dividing the
        Territories into two jurisdictions.

4-54   Constitutional Alliance of the Northwest Territories. (1988, April 30). Northern
        Decisions, 6(2), 14.

        Announcement of the agreement between the Nunavut Constitutional
        Forum (NCF) and the Western Constitutional Forum (WCF), to work
        together as a single organization responsible for constitutional development
        in the Northwest Territories.

4-55   Constitutional Alliance of the Northwest Territories (1988). <u>Progress Report,</u>
        <u>January 1987-October 1988</u>. Yellowknife, N.W.T.: Government of the
        Northwest Territories.

        Tabled document no. 6-88(2) tabled on October 14, 1988. This report
        covers the Iqaluit Agreement of 1987, the merger of the Nunavut and
        Western Constitutional Forums to form the Constitutional Alliance of the
        Northwest Territories, and progress of landclaim settlements.

4-56   <u>A Contract Relating to the Implementation of the Nunavut Final Agreement</u>.
        (1993). Ottawa, Ont.: Indian and Northern Affairs Canada.

        A contract relating to the implementation of the Nunavut final agreement
        between the Inuit of the Nunavut Settlement Area as represented by the
        Tungavik Federation of Nunavut (Inuit) and the Government of Canada, as
        represented by the Minister of Indian Affairs and Northern Development
        (Government of Canada) and the Government of the Northwest Territories
        as represented by the Minister responsible for Intergovernmental and
        Aboriginal Affairs (Territorial Government).

4-57   Coolican Report Gets Support From Both Territorial Govt.'s. (1986, June).
        <u>Building Blocks</u>, (2), 5-6.

        Comment by Yukon and Northwest Territories ministers on the Coolican
        task force recommendations, with a list of Dene/Metis and Inuit Claims sub-
        agreements to date, and chart of the comprehensive claims process.

4-58   COPE Agrees to Work With Nunavut. (1983, March). <u>Inuvialuit</u>, 3-4.

        Announcement that the Committee For Original Peoples' Entitlement
        (COPE) will work with the Nunavut Constitutional Forum (NCF) in
        working out forms of government such as the Western Arctic Regional
        Municipality (W.A.R.M.).

4-59   Cournoyea, N. J. (1990). <u>Northern Accord: Minister's Statement</u>. Yellowknife,
        N.W.T.: s.n.

        Tabled document no. 39-90(2) tabled on October 26, 1990. Statement by
        the Minister of Energy, Mines and Petroleum Resources, Northwest
        Territories, on the position of aboriginal organizations on the Northern
        Accord (under which the federal government of Canada cedes control of
        onshore oil and gas resources to the territorial government).

4-60   Cozzetto, D. (1992). Financing Aboriginal Government: The Case of Canada's
        Eastern Arctic. <u>American Indian Culture and Research Journal</u>, 16(1), 87-
        109.

        This paper seeks to develop a series of financial strategies that may assist
        those native groups involved in continued program operations as well as
        those currently negotiating aboriginal claims agreements such as Nunavut.

4-61   Creating Nunavut and Breaking the Mold of the Past. (1993, September). Northern Perspectives, 21(3), 1-8.

Account of the signing of the Nunavut Agreement, with a summary of the main features of this "modern treaty", and speeches by Paul Quassa, (President of Nunavut Tungavik Inc.), Brian Mulroney (former Prime Minister of Canada), Tom Siddon (former Minister of Indian Affairs and Northern Development), Nellie Cournoyea (Leader, Government of the Northwest Territories), and Annie Aningmiuq (Nunavut Youth Representative). Also includes commentary by Members of Parliament and Senators.

4-62   Crombie, D. (1986). [Letter to T. M. McMillan]. Ottawa, Ont.

Letter from the Minister of Indian Affairs and Northern Development to the Minister of Environment, urging acceptance of a solution to federal difficulties with the Wildlife Agreement-in-Principle negotiated with the Tungavik Federation of Nunavut (TFN) in 1981, and initialed and ratified by the TFN.

4-63   Curley, T. (1983). Policy Issues in Nunavut. Inter-Nord, (16), 407-411.

Outline of the main activities of the Inuit Tapirisat of Canada, by its chairman, and discussion of reasons for the establishment of Nunavut.

4-64   Dacks, G. (1986, March). The Case Against Dividing the Northwest Territories. Canadian Public Policy, 12(1), 202-213.

Paper argues that division of the N.W.T would divide the Inuit people, weaken the political position of other N.W.T native people, delay devolution of power northward, and impair the effectiveness and responsiveness of northern public administration.

4-65   Dacks, G. (1990). Devolution and Political Development in the Canadian North. In G. Dacks (Editor), Devolution and Constitutional Development in the Canadian North, (pp. 335- 364). Ottawa, Ont.: Carleton University Press.

Discusses implications of power transfer from Canadian federal government to governments of the Northwest Territories and Yukon for political change in the Territories.

4-66   Dacks, G. (1986, December). Reply to Richard Salisbury's Comment on "The Case Against Dividing the Northwest Territories." Canadian Public Policy, 12(4), 645-647.

"... I share [R. Salisbury's] conviction that more localized service delivery will be more responsive and contribute more to community development than does the present system. I also agree that a public service whose qualifications for employment give more emphasis to locally available skills and less to the skills stressed in southern Canadian labor market will contribute more to the satisfaction with government and prosperity of most of the communities in the Territories. However, what Salisbury does not consider is that his proposals for reform could be applied as plausibly to a fundamentally reformed government of a united N.W.T. as to the public administration of Nunavut. ..." (Author).

4-67   Dene and Metis Comprehensive Land Claim. (1990). Information Sheet (Canada. Indian and Northern Affairs Canada), 1990:22. Ottawa, Ont.: Indian and Northern Affairs Canada.

Outline of the comprehensive landclaim filed by the Dene and Metis peoples of the western part of the Northwest Territories (Mackenzie Valley).

4-68   Dene Declaration: Statement of Rights. (1975). s.l.: s.n.

Statement by the Dene (Indians) of the Northwest Territories on their right to self-determination and recognition as a nation, rather than as a group within the "Fourth World".

4-69   Dene / Metis Throw Out Overlap Agreement: Boundary Lines Are Needed For Both Claims and Division. (1987, April). Nunavut, 6(4), 2-6.

Discussion of the announcement by the Dene / Metis Negotiating Secretariat that they were withdrawing support of the May 1984 Overlap Agreement with the Inuvialiut, and the May 1988 Overlap Agreement with the Inuit, on the boundary lines of Nunavut, Denendeh and the Inuvialuit Settlement Region.

4-70   Dene Nation. (1987, December 15). Northern Decisions, 5(16), 141.

Notice of meeting between landclaims negotiators for the Dene/Metis and the Tungavik Federation of Nunavut, in Yellowknife, Northwest Territories, to discuss resuming talks on the overlapping claims boundary.

4-71   Dene Nation and Metis Association of the Northwest Territories (1988). Devolution of Powers to the Government of the Northwest Territories: Provincehood and Aboriginal Self- Government. Yellowknife, N.W.T.: Dene Nation.

This document sets out the position of the Dene, Metis and Inuit peoples of the Northwest Territories with regard to native self-government, a constitution for the Northwest Territories and the state of the Constitutional Alliance.

4-72   Dene Nation and the Metis Association of the Northwest Territories (1988). Presentation on Constitutional and Political Development to the Legislative Assembly of the Northwest Territories. Yellowknife, N.W.T.: Government of the Northwest Territories.

This paper deals with the position of the Dene Nation and the Metis Association of the Northwest Territories on aboriginal self-government and on constitutional change, as in particular public participation in the decision-making process, changes in electoral boundaries and the number of seats in the Legislative Assembly.

4-73   Development Impact: Screening and Assessment of Project Proposals and
        Applications, Provisions of an Agreement-in-Principle. (1985). Calgary,
        Alta.: Tungavik Federation of Nunavut.

        Text of the Tungavik Federation of Nunavut (TFN) position on some
        provisions of an Agreement-in-Principle (to form part of the Nunavut Land
        Claims Settlement) on screening and assessment of project proposals as an
        integral part of offshore management.

4-74   Development Impact: Screening and Review. (1990). Yellowknife, N.W.T.:
        Government of the Northwest Territories.

        Explanation of the role and functions of the Nunavut Impact Review Board,
        created under the Agreement-in-Principle which determined the boundaries
        of Nunavut, the Inuit subdivision of the Northwest Territories. The Board
        (or NIRB) intends to protect the "ecosystemic integrity" of the area, to
        monitor the environmental impacts of resource development and
        conservation, to review proposed land use changes, and to promote the
        existing and future well-being of the residents and communities of Nunavut.

4-75   Devine, M. (1992, June). Building Nunavut. Up-Here, 8(3), 18-21.

        Discussion of the form and style of government, civil service, economy, and
        society expected to develop in Nunavut.

4-76   Devine, M. (1992, January). Good-bye to the Three-Legged Polar Bear. Arctic
        Circle, 2(4), 18-19.

        Commentary on the impact of the probable creation of Nunavut, on the
        economy and government of the Northwest Territories.

4-77   Devolution? Division? Land Claims? One Won't Happen Without The Other
        Two: Crombie. (1986, January). Nunavut, 5(1), 2.

        Discussion of the devolution of powers to the territorial government of the
        Northwest Territories and its effects on division and landclaims in Nunavut.

4-78   Dickerson, M. O., & McCullough, K. M. (1993, June). Nunavut ("Our Land").
        Information North, 19(2), 1-7.

        Brief historical account of the creation of Nunavut and basic information on
        the Agreement-in-Principle. Includes map and chronology.

4-79   Doering, R. L. (1992, January). In Politics, As in Comedy, Timing is Everything.
        Arctic Circle, 2(4), 17.

        Commentary on timing and significance of the landclaim and Nunavut
        negotiations, for the north and Canada in general.

4-80   Doering, R. L. (1983). Nunavut and Land Claims: Options for a Public Land Regime. Working Paper, 3. Ottawa, Ont.: Nunavut Constitutional Forum.

Explores the problems of linking Tungavik Federation of Nunavut landclaims with the Inuit Tapirisat of Canada proposal for the creation of Nunavut.

4-81   Dogrib and Chipewyan Land Use in the Dene/Inuit Overlap Region. (1985). Edmonton, Alta.: Dene Mapping Project.

This compilation of land use maps focuses on traplines and trails used by hunters and trappers in the area northeast of Yellowknife, Northwest Territories, in which Dene landclaims overlap with those of Inuit claims in the Nunavut area.

4-82   Dufton, R. (1986, May). Offshore Bill May Complicate Land Claims. Nunavut, 5(5), 4.

Explanation of amendments to the proposed Canada Laws Offshore Application Act (defining the boundaries of the Northwest Territories) which the Tungavik Federation of Nunavut feels are necessary to support Inuit hunting rights.

4-83   Dufton, R. (1987, June). Policies are Inconsistent, Says TFN. Nunavut, 6(6), 6.

Summary of Inuit concerns about the Federal Government's Northern Mineral Policy for increased exploration and mining.

4-84   East and West Agree on Tentative Boundary. (1985, March). Nunavut, 4(2), 2.

Announcement of provisional agreement on the boundary between Nunavut and the western part of the Northwest Territories as negotiated by the Constitutional Alliance. Includes map of disputed areas.

4-85   Eetoolook, J. (1993, March). TFN 1992 Report. Nunavut, 12(2), 1.

Summary of the activities and achievements of the Tungavik Federation of Nunavut (TFN) in 1992, including signing of the Political Accord in Iqaluit, the incorporation of Tungavik Inc., and the Nunavut Trust.

4-86   Eetoolook, J., & Pilakapsi, P. K. (1992). Dear Fellow Inuk. Ottawa, Ont.: Nunavut Land Claims.

Text of a letter from the presidents of the Tungavik Federation of Nunavut and the Kitikmeot, Keewatin, and Baffin Region Inuit Associations to all Inuit, concerning the Nunavut Land Claim Agreement, its terms and the ratification process leading to the establishment of the government of Nunavut.

4-87 Eligibility Criteria of Other Agreements: Background Information for TFN
Discussion on Enrollment and Eligibility. (1986). Ottawa, Ont.: Tungavik
Federation of Nunavut.

This document is based on information in TFN research files and compiles
the requirements for eligibility (to receive rights and benefits) from
landclaim agreements in northern Canada. It is intended to assist in defining
eligibility in the Nunavut claim area.

4-88 Elliott, R. (1990, December). Wildlife Managers Greet 1990 With New
Management Board. Nunavut, 9(1), 11-13.

Explanation of the structure and functions of the Nunavut Wildlife
Management Advisory Board.

4-89 Enerk, P. (1987, January). Offshore Resources Become Food on Our Tables.
Nunavut, 6(1), 6-7.

Statement of the importance of offshore resources to the Inuit of the
Hudson Bay in relation to proposed industrial development.

4-90 Enrollment and Eligibility Update. (1991, July). Nunavut, 10(2), 24.

Explanation of how to enroll and who is eligible for voting in the
ratification vote on the Nunavut Land Claims Agreement, and the role of the
Community Enrollment Committee (CEC).

4-91 Enrollment Must be Fair, Accurate and Complete. (1985, November). Nunavut,
4(6), 6.

Summary of how the Tungavik Federation of Nunavut (TFN) will proceed
on questions of eligibility and enrollment in Nunavut.

4-92 An Estimate of Costs - Creating and Operating the Government of Nunavut.
(1992). Ottawa, Ont.: Dept. of Indian and Northern Development.

Tabled document no. 75-12(3) tabled on March 2, 1993. Document setting
out probable costs in financial and personnel terms, of setting up and
delivering government services in the new Inuit Territory of Nunavut
(eastern Northwest Territories), to the year 2004.

4-93 Feds Break Word. (1983, February). Nunavut Newsletter, 3.

Statement that the Wildlife Agreement-in-Principle may be altered without
consultation with Inuit leaders.

4-94 Fenge, T. (1987, March). Conserving Nunavut Through the Settlement of the
Inuit Land Claim. Park News, 23(1), 35-40.

This article shows how the settlement of the Inuit landclaim can be used to
conserve the natural resources of the eastern and central arctic.

4-95   Fenge, T. (1991, August). Land Selection Negotiations Completed Nunavut Wide. Nunavut, 10(3), 6.

Announcement of the completion of land ownership negotiations in the Kitikmeot region of the Northwest Territories by the Tungavik Federation of Nunavut.

4-96   Fenge, T. (1991, December). The Nunavut Final Agreement. Nunavut, 11(1), 6-8.

Summary of the contents and significance of the Nunavut Final Agreement, on creation of the new jurisdiction, to be ratified in November 1992.

4-97   Fenge, T. (1992). Political Development and Environmental Management in Northern Canada: the Case of the Nunavut Agreement. Etudes Inuit Studies, 16(1-2), 115-141.

Begins with a brief overview of how the Nunavut Agreement fits into the historical development of land rights of aboriginal inhabitants and the federal government's policy on comprehensive landclaims. The negotiating process on the part of the Inuit and federal government is summarized and management of wildlife, land, freshwater and oceans to be conducted by institutions established pursuant to the agreement is discussed. Includes a section on the author's personal observations on how it proved possible for the Inuit to overcome various barriers to conclude the agreement.

4-98   Fenge, T. (1991, October). Ratifying the Nunavut Final Agreement. Nunavut, 10(4), 12.

Progress report on the work of the Ratification Committee on the vote on approval of the Nunavut Final Agreement in 1992.

4-99   Fenge, T. (1986, March). TFN Says "No" To New Parks Without WAIP Endorsement. Nunavut, 8(3), 3.

Withdrawal of support by Tungavik Federation of Nunavut for new national parks, national wildlife areas, and migratory bird sanctuaries in Nunavut, until the Federal Department of Environment ratifies the Wildlife Agreement-in-Principle initialed in 1981.

4-100   Fenge, T. (1991, December). Vote "Yes" on the Boundary For Nunavut. Nunavut, 11(1), 10.

Summary of the purpose and significance of the plebiscite of May 4, 1992 on the boundary of Nunavut and the rest of the Northwest Territories.

4-101   Fenge, T., & Barnaby, J. (1987, January). From Recommendations to Policy: Battling Inertia to Obtain a Land Claims Policy. Northern Perspectives, 15(1), 12-15.

The authors describe the claims coalition formed in April 1986 to press the federal government for a new policy based on recommendations of the Coolican report.

4-102   Final Results of Tungavik Federation of Nunavut (TFN) Ratification Vote.
         (1992). Yellowknife, N.W.T.: Government of the Northwest Territories.

         Tabled document tabled on November 17, 1992. Results by region (Baffin,
         Keewatin, Kitikmeot) for the TFN Land Claim, and statement of votes cast.

4-103   Flaherty, M. (1987, October). Artifacts Tell Stories About the Past. Nunavut,
         6(8), 8.

         Note on the agreement between the Tungavik Federation of Nunavut and
         Federal Government of Canada on control and management of
         archaeological sites and artifacts.

4-104   Flaherty, M. (1986, March). Here is a Review of Northern Land Use Planning.
         Nunavut, 5(3), 2.

         Summary of the how and why of land use planning in the Northwest
         Territories, including the Policy Advisory Committee and the Land Use
         Planning Commission, and its relations with the Tungavik Federation of
         Nunavut.

4-105   Flaherty, M. (1985, November). Nunavut is Still a Dream. Nunavut, 4(6), 5.

         Summary of the meeting in Coppermine, Northwest Territories, on
         September 25-27, 1985, at which the Nunavut Constitutional Forum
         decided to hold a plebiscite to determine the public will regarding Nunavut

4-106   Foster, M. (1984). A Natural Boundary to Divide the Northwest Territories.
         Yellowknife, N.W.T.: Northern Canada Power Commission.

         This paper argues that the "straight-line" approach to a boundary between
         the eastern and western sections of the Northwest Territories will inevitably
         create innumerable problems concerning the allocation and use of natural
         resources between the new jurisdictions, and recommends using the
         watershed boundary between Hudson Bay and the Mackenzie Basin as the
         dividing line between east and west N.W.T.

4-107   Gillies, B. (1991, October). Conclusion of Land Ownership Negotiations.
         Nunavut, 10(4), 8.

         Commentary on the Tungavik Federation of Nunavut Land Identification
         Project of 1988-1991.

4-108   "A Good Track Record": Says Chief Negotiator. (1986, October). Nunavut,
         5(10), 4.

         Discussion of progress to date on the landclaims settlement for Nunavut.

4-109   Government Announces New Claims Policy: a Summary. (1987, February).
         Nunavut, 6(2), 2-3.

         Summary of content and scope of the new Federal Government policy on
         landclaims, including alternatives to extinguishment, negotiation of
         management roles, profit sharing, and land ownership. Also reminds readers
         of the initialing of two sub-agreements at Cambridge Bay, N.W.T., in April
         1983: Purpose of Inuit Land Title, and: Principles to Guide Inuit Land
         Identification.

4-110   Government Approves Federal Mandate for TFN Claim. (1988, January).
         Nunavut, 7(1), 2-3.

         Explanation of content of the new Federal Government policy on settlement
         of landclaims and its effect on the progress of the Inuit claim.

4-111   Government Cannot Limit Aboriginal Rights. (1988, June). Nunavut, 7(5), 4.

         Discussion of the effect of Bill C-30 (an amendment to the National Parks
         Act, Canada) on Inuit hunting, fishing and trapping rights in Nunavut.

4-112   Government Committee Listens to Inuit Side of Story. (1986, September).
         Nunavut, 5(9), 5.

         Statement by Peter Ernerk, board member of the Tungavik Federation of
         Nunavut, to the Federal Standing committee on Indian Affairs and Northern
         Development, on the meaning and importance of wildlife to Inuit.

4-113   Government Has One Policy But Many Pairs of "Eyes". (1986, November).
         Nunavut, 5(11), 4.

         Presentation by Tom Molloy, direct negotiator for the Federal Government,
         to the Board of the Tungavik Federation of Nunavut, at Igloolik in October
         1986, on progress in landclaim negotiations.

4-114   Government of the Northwest Territories, Financial Impact of Division. (1991).
         Edmonton, Alta.: Coopers and Lybrand.

         This study attempts to develop accurate financial projections of the costs
         and funding arrangements necessary to support two governments in the
         Northwest Territories, following the proposed division into Nunavut
         (eastern Territories) and Denendeh (western portion) and assuming
         maintenance of the current level of public sector services.

4-115   Government of the Northwest Territories. (1976?). Brief of the Government of
         the Northwest Territories to the Honourable Judd Buchanan on the Inuit
         Land Claims Proposal "Nunavut". Yellowknife, N.W.T.: Government of the
         Northwest Territories.

         Statement of the position of the territorial council on the "Nunavut"
         proposal by ITC (Inuit Tapirisat of Canada), in a brief to the Minister of
         Indian Affairs and Northern Development.

4-116   Government Proposes Changes to Wildlife Agreement-in-Principle. (1983, August). <u>Nunavut Newsletter</u>, 11-12.

    Discussion of changes proposed by the Federal Government of Canada to the Wildlife Agreement-in-Principle for Nunavut.

4-117   <u>Guide to the Tungavik Federation of Nunavut Land Claim Agreement-In-Principle</u>. (1990). Ottawa, Ont.: Indian and Northern Affairs Canada.

    Brief guide to the general provisions of the agreement-in-principle made by the Tungavik Federation of Nunavut to settle Inuit landclaims in the Northwest Territories. Includes map of boundaries.

4-118   Gunther, M. (1991). <u>The Boundary and Overlap Negotiations of the Tungavik Federation of Nunavut and the Dene/Metis Negotiations Secretariat: the Present Position of the Parties</u>. Ottawa, Ont.: Dept. of Indian Affairs and Northern Development.

    Report of the fact-finder appointed by the Minister of Indian Affairs and Northern Development, to attempt to define the latest boundaries of lands in Manitoba and the Northwest Territories claimed by both Inuit and Dene/Metis groups as traditional hunting areas, in order to clarify the boundary dispute before implementation of self-government in the Northwest Territories.

4-119   Hawkes, D. C. (1989). <u>Aboriginal Peoples and Constitutional Reform: What Have We Learned? : Phase Three, Final Report</u>. Kingston, Ont.: Queen's University, Institute of Intergovernmental Relations.

    A study of aboriginal self-government (for Indian, Inuit, and Metis groups) in Canada and discussion as to why constitutional reform has not been achieved in this area since the Constitution Act (1982) up to the Meech Lake Accord in 1989.

4-120   Hawkes, D. C. (1985). Negotiating Aboriginal Self-Government. In P. M. Leslie (Editor), <u>Canada: the State of the Federation</u>, (pp. 151-172). Kingston, Ont.: Queen's University.

    An examination of recent negotiations on aboriginal self-government, concentrating analysis on developments which have occurred since the election of the Progressive Conservative federal government in September 1984.

4-121   Haysom, V., & Richstone, J. (1987). Customizing Law in the Territories: Proposal For a Task Force on Customary Law in Nunavut. <u>Etudes/Inuit Studies</u>, 11(1), 91-106.

    Brief summary of recent constitutional developments in the Northwest Territories, focusing on problems for a task force to consider in implementing Inuit customary law.

4-122   High Arctic Tour Takes Unexpected Turn. (1984, October). <u>Nunavut Newsletter</u>, 3(8), 2-3.

Report on requests by High Arctic communities for continuing information on the Nunavut landclaim negotiations.

4-123   Hunters in Nunavut and Quebec Need Common Rules. (1985, May). <u>Nunavut</u>, 4(3), 3.

Announcement of a plan for the Tungavik Federation of Nunavut, and Makivik (northern Quebec) to work towards agreement on common rules for use of wildlife in Hudson Bay and the Hudson Strait Islands.

4-124   <u>Impasse Resolved on Wildlife Provision in Inuit Land Claim: Draft</u>. (1986). Ottawa, Ont.: Minister of Indian Affairs and Northern Development.

Announcement by the Minister of Indian Affairs and Northern Development that he and the Minster of Fisheries and Oceans, and the Minister of Environment, have agreed to proposals that will end a four year impasse over the Wildlife Provisions of an Agreement-in-Principle negotiated with the Tungavik Federation of Nunavut (TFN).

4-125   Implementation Plan Will Lift Words Off Paper! (1988, September). <u>Nunavut</u>, 7(7), 2.

Explanation of the Implementation Plan for the Final Agreement on Nunavut: guidelines for the operation of a Nunavut Wildlife Management Advisory Board (including implementation by a Working Group before settlement of the entire claim): initialing of the Arbitration Provisions of an Agreement-in-Principle, dealing with interpretation and implementation problems and setting up an Arbitration Board.

4-126   <u>Income Security Program for Inuit Harvesters: Economic Resources Package Discussion Paper</u>. (1987). s.l.: s.n.

This paper presents the rationale and mechanisms for income supplementation to Inuit hunters and trappers in the Nunavut claim area as a means of sustaining the traditional land-based economy.

4-127   An Interview With Paul Quassa: "Money is Not Our Number One Priority". (1990, December). <u>Nunavut</u>, 9(1), 4-6.

Discussion of the terms and significance of the Nunavut Land Claim Agreement-in-Principle, with the Chief Negotiator for the Tungavik Federation of Nunavut, Paul Quaasa.

4-128   <u>An Introduction Paper for the Discussion of the Negotiation of Social Provisions</u>. (1986). Ottawa, Ont.: Tungavik Federation of Nunavut.

This paper is intended to provide the Tungavik Federation of Nunavut research/negotiation team with an overview of general points to consider when developing an approach to the negotiation of social provisions for the Nunavut claim.

4-129 The Inuit. (1990). Information Sheet (Canada. Indian and Northern Affairs Canada), 1990:16. Ottawa, Ont.: Indian and Northern Affairs Canada.

Brief history and account of current life style and issues such as landclaims (for Nunavut) of the Inuit in the Northwest Territories.

4-130 Inuit and the Constitutional Referendum on the Charlottetown Accord: Vote on October 26. (1992). Ottawa, Ont.: Inuit Tapirisat of Canada.

Summary of the position of the Inuit Tapirisat of Canada on the Charlottetown Accord (agreement for constitutional renewal) of 1992, and results of the Pangnitung Accord 1991/1992 (Inuit Assembly on the Charlottetown Accord).

4-131 Inuit Committee on National Issues (1987). Completing Canada: Inuit Approaches to Self-Government. Aboriginal Peoples and Constitutional Reform. Position paper. Kingston, Ont.: Institute of Intergovernmental Relations, Queen's University.

Summarizes views presented in previous research studies and position papers, speeches, briefs and other documents prepared by the Inuit Committee on National Issues and various regional Inuit organizations.

4-132 Inuit Cultural Institute Helps TFN. (1986, September). Nunavut, 5(9), 4.

Report on progress made by the Inuit Cultural Institute in implementing provisions of the archaeology sub-agreement, initialed in 1983, for creation of the Inuit Heritage Trust.

4-133 Inuit Get Landmark Agreement on Offshore. (1988, March). Nunavut, 7(3), 2-7.

Outline of the provisions of an Agreement-in-Principle on Marine Areas, which includes Inuit rights to the use of offshore areas and resources under a marine management system and provision for a clause on "Wildlife Management and Harvesting beyond the Marine areas of the Claim".

4-134 Inuit Impact and Benefit Agreements: TFN Position. (1984). Ottawa, Ont.: Tungavik Federation of Nunavut.

Summary of the position of the Tungavik Federation of Nunavut on Inuit Impact and Benefit Agreements as they would relate to major development proposals in the Nunavut claim area.

4-135 Inuit Involvement in the Selection, Establishment, Use, Management and Planning of National Parks in Inuit Nunangat: Draft.--. (1988). Yellowknife, N.W.T.: Inuit Tapirisat of Canada.

This draft proposal by the Inuit Tapirisat of Canada seeks funds to support a study of six proposed National Parks within the area of the Northwest Territories and Quebec affected by Inuit land claims (Inuit Nunangat), and of the ways in which consultation with Inuit groups can take place on legal and management issues.

4-136   Inuit Land Identification Process. (1986). Ottawa, Ont.: s.n.

Draft of provisions for identification of Inuit Lands in the Nunavut Claim Area, dated December 10, 1986.

4-137   The Inuit: Moving Slowly Toward Nunavut. (1984, December). Project North Journal, 8(1), 4.

Summary of the current state of negotiations on the Nunavut landclaim.

4-138   Inuit Must be Equal Partners. (1987, June). Nunavut, 6(6), 5.

Report of progress in reaching a Northern Energy Accord on management and revenue sharing related to mineral, oil and gas development, between the Federal Government of Canada and the Northwest Territories.

4-139   Inuit Negotiate Agreement on National Parks. (1983, August). Nunavut Newsletter, 8-10.

Provisions of the Agreement-in-Principle on national Parks in Nunavut, including IIBAs (Inuit Impact and Benefit Agreements) and a map.

4-140   Inuit Owned Lands: Nunavut. (1993, May). Nunavut, 12(3), 6.

Map of the Nunavut Settlement Area including: High Arctic area exempt from Inuit land ownership, Inuit-owned lands, and Crown (public) lands, with reference to relevant sections of the Nunavut Final Agreement.

4-141   Inuit Sub-Agreements. (1986, August). Building Blocks, (4), 5.

List to date of Inuit and Dene/Metis Sub-Agreements initialed for landclaims.

4-142   Inuit Tell TFN to Begin Land Ownership Talks. (1987, November). Nunavut, 6(9), 2.

Report of tours of communities in the Northwest Territories by negotiators from the Tungavik Federation of Nunavut to seek Inuit opinion on the mechanism for identifying Inuit-owned land.

4-143   Inuit Will Control Who Goes on Their Land. (1987, October). Nunavut, 6(8), 2.

Announcement of the initialing of an agreement-in-principle, on entry and access to and across Inuit lands, for general, government and third party access.

4-144   Inuit Will Guide Use of Land in Nunavut. (1984, August). <u>Nunavut Newsletter,</u> 3(6), 2-4.

Outline of the provisions for land use planning in Nunavut as agreed to by the Tungavik Federation of Nunavut (TFN) and the Federal Government of Canada.

4-145   Inuit Will Share Benefits of Development. (1985, February). <u>Nunavut,</u> 5(2), 3.

Announcement of initialing of provisions for "Inuit Impact and Benefit Agreements" (IIBAs) and explanation of how they will relate to the Nunavut Impact Review Board (NIRB).

4-146   Inuktitut is Contemporary Language at TFN. (1985, December). <u>Uqaqta,</u> (2), 2-4.

Commentary on the use of Inuktitut in the proposed Nunavut claims settlement.

4-147   Ipellie, A. (1991, August). Carrying the Nunavut Torch. <u>Nunavut,</u> 10(3), 4.

Announcement of the signing of an agreement between the Tungavik Federation of Nunavut and Minister of Indian Affairs and Northern Development on the western boundary of Nunavut.

4-148   Ipellie, A. (1991, October). Inuit Customary Law and the Canadian Constitution. <u>Nunavut,</u> 10(4), 1-6.

Comparison of traditional law and legal concepts of the Inuit, and Canadian law and constitution in the context of Nunavut and aboriginal self-government.

4-149   Ipellie, A. (1991, July). You Can Make a Difference. <u>Nunavut,</u> 10(2), 23.

Commentary on the progress and history of the Inuit Tapirisat of Canada and Tungavik Federation of Nunavut, in their 20th anniversary year.

4-150   Irwin, C. (1989). <u>Lords of the Arctic: Wards of the State: the Growing Inuit Population, Arctic Resettlement and Their Effects on Social and Economic Change</u>. Halifax, N.S.: Dalhousie University, Dept. of Sociology and Social Anthropology.

Attempts to describe the social and economic changes brought about by the resettlement of Inuit into villages in the late 1950's and early 1960's and by the growth of the Inuit population in the Canadian Arctic.

4-151   Irwin, C., & Malone, M. (1989). Lords of the Arctic: Wards of the State: The Growing Inuit Population, Arctic Resettlement, and Their Effects on Social and Economic Change: A Summary Report. <u>Northern Perspectives,</u> 17(1), 1-20.

Contains shortened version of Irwin's "Lords of the Arctic" report on the future of the Inuit, together with responses on behalf of the Government of N.W.T. and the Tungavik Federation of Nunavut and Irwin's reply to these responses.

4-152   Isaac, T. (1992, March). The Nunavut Agreement-in-Principle and Section 35 of the Constitution Act, 1982. Manitoba Law Journal, 21(3), 390-405.

This paper examines the Nunavut Agreement-in-Principle as a constitutional document as it relates to the Canadian Charter of Rights and Freedoms, and the Constitution Act 1982, and suggests some possible amendments that could maximize the constitutional implications of the Agreement-in-Principle.

4-153   J. Mark Stiles & Associates (1984). Nunavut Aulatsininga (Managing Nunavut): an Action Proposal for an Inuit Management Development and Training Strategy in Preparation for Nunavut and a Land Claims Settlement. Ottawa, Ont.: Inuit Tapirisat of Canada.

The success of Nunavut, the name for the proposed system of northern self-government, depends on the availability of Inuit who possess the necessary training and experience for key business and government jobs. To this end, the consultant's report suggests that a training program be set up in connection with the Arctic College system.

4-154   Joint Discussion Paper Regarding Equity Participation in Onshore Oil and Gas. (1986). Ottawa, Ont.: Tungavik Federation of Nunavut?

This paper explores matters related to oil and gas exploration and production on lands within the Nunavut claim area in terms of equity for the Tungavik Federation of Nunavut and the Federal Government of Canada.

4-155   Jull, P. (1983, February). Building Nunavut. Nunavut Newsletter, 4.

Discussion by the research coordinator for the Nunavut Constitutional Forum, of the history of the Nunavut idea, and of how a constitution for Nunavut will be developed. Also describes the ICNI (Inuit Committee On National Issues).

4-156   Jull, P. (1985, December). Gordon Robertson Says: Provincehood is a Mistaken Goal. Nunavut, 4(7), 8.

Views expressed by Gordon Robertson, former Commissioner of the Northwest Territories, on whether provincehood is desirable for Nunavut.

4-157   Jull, P. (1990). Inuit Concerns and Environmental Assessment. In D. L. VanderZwaag, & C. Lamson (Editors), The Challenge of Arctic Shipping: Science, Environmental Assessment, and Human Values. McGill-Queen's Series in Northern and Native Studies 2, (pp. 139-153). Montreal, Que.: McGill-Queen's University Press.

Discussion of the Inuit and non-northern approach to environmental concerns, including proposed oil development in Lancaster Sound and Inuit rights to the use of ocean areas in the Northwest Territories, including Nunavut, with a comparison to the Alaska North Slope, and Greenland.

4-158   Jull, P. (1984, November). Nunavut and Regionalism. Inuit, The Magazine of the Inuit Circumpolar Conference, 11.

Discussion of the type of government suited to Nunavut.

4-159   Jull, P. (1987). Nunavut: Self-Government and Arctic Sovereignty: a Background Paper For the Nunavut Constitutional Forum. Ottawa, Ont.: Nunavut Constitutional Forum.

Discussion of the continued need for creation of Nunavut following the Meech Lake Accord of 1987, as a means of domestic government and assertion of Canadian Arctic sovereignty, with emphasis on process rather than immediate change.

4-160   Jull, P., & Bankes, N. (1984). Inuit Interests in the Arctic Offshore. In National Workshop on People, Resources and the Environment North of 60 (3rd: 1983: Yellowknife, N.W.T.), Ocean Policy and Management in the Arctic, (pp. 83-114). Ottawa, Ont.: Canadian Arctic Resources Committee.

This paper examines the legal basis of an aboriginal offshore claim in the Canadian Arctic, the political context of aboriginal claims (the Northwest Territories context and the Canadian/international context). Against the imbalance between aboriginal and federal negotiating positions, a functional resolution would take into account the proposals set forth by the Tungavik Federation of Nunavut.

4-161   Kadlun, B. (1987, January). Chief Negotiator Explains Claim to Geo-Science Forum. Nunavut, 6(1), 5-6.

Explanation of the basic issues of concern to the Tungavik Federation of Nunavut (TFN) in settling Inuit claims: the offshore, a co-management role for Inuit and guarantees for economic self-sufficiency.

4-162   Kakfwi, S. (1991). Aboriginal People's Inherent Right to Self Government. Yellowknife, N.W.T.: Government of the Northwest Territories.

Tabled document no. 21-12(1) tabled on December 17, 1991. Statement by Stephen Kakfwi, Minister of Intergovernmental and Aboriginal Affairs, Northwest Territories, on the right to self-government of aboriginal peoples, with reference to the Gwich'in Final Claim Agreement.

4-163   Kakfwi, S. (1992). Nunavut Political Accord Ratification. Yellowknife, N.W.T.: Government of the Northwest Territories.

Tabled document no. 84-12(2) tabled on September 10, 1992. Announcement by the Minister for Intergovernmental and Aboriginal Affairs, Northwest Territories (Stephen Kakfwi) of the approval by the Cabinet of the Federal Government of Canada, of the Nunavut Political Accord (Nunavut Agreement), and the appointment of the Nunavut Implementation Commission to oversee the creation of Nunavut by 1999.

4-164 Kakfwi, S. (1991). TFN Claim. Yellowknife, N.W.T.: Government of the Northwest Territories.

Tabled document no.19-12(1) tabled on December 16, 1991. Announcement by Stephen Kakfwi, Minister of Intergovernmental and Aboriginal Affairs, Northwest Territories, of the successful conclusion of landclaim negotiations between the Federal government and the Tungavik Federation of Nunavut (TFN).

4-165 Keenleyside, A. H. (1985). Notarial Copy of Signed Original of TFN/COPE Agreement dated May 19, 1984, With Descriptions of Original and Adjusted Boundaries. Ottawa, Ont.: Anthony Keenleyside.

Text of the Agreement between the Tungavik Federation of Nunavut (TFN) and the Committee For Original Peoples' Entitlement (COPE), on the location of the boundary between the Western Arctic and Nunavut claims, and on the status of residents of Holman. Includes map and legal description.

4-166 Kelly, P. (1991). Baffin Regional AIP Workshop. Nunavut, 10(2), 25.

Explanation of how to enroll and who is eligible for voting in the ratification vote on the Nunavut Land Claims Agreement, and the role Community Enrollment Committees (CEC).

4-167 Kerr, K. (1991, August). Negotiations on South Baffin Land. Nunavut, 10(3), 8.

Account of negotiations between the Community Land Identification Negotiation Team (CLINT) and the Federal Government, on Inuit control of Pangnirtung Pass, Baffin Island.

4-168 Kerr, K. (1991, August). Negotiations on Municipal Lands in South Baffin. Nunavut, 10(3), 10-12.

Details of consultations between the Community Lands Identification Negotiating Team (CLINT) and the Federal Government on lands in the Iqaluit - Apex area, Baffin Island.

4-169 KIA on Offshore. (1984, December). Nunavut, 3(10), 2.

Resolution by the KIA (Keewatin Inuit Association) urging the Federal Government and Tungavik Federation of Nunavut to ensure that the offshore resources of Hudson Bay are protected in the landclaim settlement.

4-170 Land Claims Negotiations Will Resume. (1983, March). Nunavut Newsletter, 2-3.

Announcement of resumption of negotiations by the Tungavik Federation of Nunavut, on economic benefits, and of support by the Northern Affairs Minister for joint management boards as part of a landclaims settlement.

4-171   Land ID Workers Face Big Challenge. (1986, October). <u>Nunavut</u>, 5(10), 9.

        Appointment of land identification field workers for the Keewatin and Baffin regions of Nunavut.

4-172   Land ID Workers Visit Two Communities. (1986, January). <u>Nunavut</u>, 5(1), 6.

        Explanation of the Land Identification Project for Nunavut, the three types of land ownership and the role of land identification workers in the communities.

4-173   Land Identification Project is Underway. (1985, November). <u>Nunavut</u>, 6(6), 9.

        Announcement of the Tungavik Federation of Nunavut's Land Identification Project to define Inuit land in the N.W.T.

4-174   Land Merges With Frozen Sea in Nunavut. (1985, June). <u>Nunavut</u>, 4(4), 2-4.

        Summary of a workshop held by the Office of Native Claims May 30-31, 1988, to consider the status and use of the offshore zone of land-locked and shore-fast ice in Nunavut.

4-175   Last Major Northern Land Claim Settled. (1990, June). <u>Arctic Petroleum Review</u>, 13(1), 3.

        Outline of the Agreement-in-Principle between the Tungavik Federation of Nunavut and the Federal Government of Canada, including agreement on subsurface mineral rights and resource royalties.

4-176   Lawrence, R. (1993, June). Our Land: Dream of Nunavut Now a Reality. <u>Transition</u>, 6(6), 1,6,8.

        Account of the signing of the Nunavut Final Agreement in Iqaluit, May 25, 1993.

4-177   Lester, G. S. (1984). <u>Inuit Territorial Rights in the Canadian Northwest Territories: a Survey of the Legal Problems</u>. Ottawa, Ont.: Tungavik Federation of Nunavut.

        Examines the traditional view of aboriginal rights of the Eskimo of the Northwest Territories. Abridged version of the author's Doctoral thesis "The Territorial Rights of the Inuit of the Canadian Northwest Territories: a Legal Argument".

4-178   <u>Letter to the Prime Minister of Canada</u>. (1990). Yellowknife, N.W.T.: Government of the Northwest Territories.

        Tabled document no. 23-90(2) tabled on October 22, 1990. Text of a letter from the Leader of the Government of the Northwest Territories and the

President of the Tungavik Federation of Nunavut to the Prime Minister of Canada, agreeing on a target date for creation of a Nunavut territory and government.

4-179   Mackay, R., & Rand, J. (1984). Cost of Implementing Inuktitut as an Official Language in Nunavut. Maxville, Ont.: R. Mackay.

The purpose of this study is to estimate the feasibility and cost of the Nunavut Constitutional Forum intention to implement Inuktitut as an official language in the proposed Nunavut territory (Building Nunavut 1983, pp. 18-19) for public services, publications, legal materials, education, the media and interpretation and translation services.

4-180   Maghagak, A. (1983, May). Chief Negotiator Reports. Nunavut Newsletter, 2.

Report of the Chief Negotiator for the Tungavik Federation of Nunavut on the questions of land identification, and the offshore and royalty rights.

4-181   Maghagak, A. (1984, March). Maghagak Looks Back in 1983 . Nunavut Newsletter, 5-6.

Summary of progress on Nunavut landclaims in 1983.

4-182   Maghagak, A. (1992, November). Nunavut, Inuit Taking Back Self-Determination. Nunavut, 11(6), 16-20.

Brief summary of terms and implications of the Nunavut Agreement as ratified in November 1992.

4-183   Maghagak Wants Strong Economy for Inuit. (1983, April). Nunavut Newsletter, 2.

Statement on the results of negotiations on economic benefits between the Federal Government of Canada and the Tungavik Federation of Nunavut.

4-184   Malone, S. M. (1983). Nunavut: Financial Perspectives. Working Paper Nunavut Constitutional Forum, 2. Ottawa, Ont.: Nunavut Constitutional Forum.

Discusses the financial aspects of the Inuit Tapirisat of Canada proposal for a separate territory north of the treeline called Nunavut.

4-185   Malone, S. M. (1987). Nunavut: The Division of Power. Working Paper Nunavut Constitutional Forum, 1. Ottawa, Ont.?: Nunavut Constitutional Forum.

Discusses the Inuit Tapirisat of Canada proposal for a separate Territory north of the treeline called Nunavut. Paper includes a framework for proposals and tentative proposals for a division of powers between the legislative bodies involved.

4-186   Managing the Future: Trustees of Land Claims Take Firm Stand to Protect
         Compensation Money. (1983, July). Nunavut Newsletter, 2-4.

         Discussion of the position of TFN (Tungavik Federation of Nunavut) on
         whether to approve a loan guarantee requested by the Nunasi Development
         Corporation.

4-187   Manitoba Indians Ask For Land North of 60. (1984, November). Nunavut,
         3(9), 4.

         Report of meeting in Thompson, Manitoba, of the Indians of Tadoule Lake,
         Manitoba and representatives of the Tungavik Federation of Nunavut, on
         the question of Indian land ownership in the Northwest Territories.

4-188   Map of the Boundary for Division as Set Out in the Plebiscite Direction and
         Proclamation, 1992 . (1992, March). Nunavut, 11(2), 6-7.

         Map of the Northwest Territories showing proposed boundary of Nunavut,
         to be the subject of a plebiscite on May 4, 1992: includes graph of results of
         1982 plebiscite.

4-189   McEwen, J. (1990, June). Celebrating an Agreement-Inuit Style. Transition,
         3(6), 1,8.

         Account of the celebration at Igloolik, N.W.T., at the signing of the
         Agreement-in-Principle for the Tungavik Federation of Nunavut Land
         Claim.

4-190   Memorandum of Understanding Between Tungavik Federation of Nunavut
         (TFN) and the Fort Churchill Band and the Northlands Band. (1986,
         August). Nunavut, 5(8), 2.

         Text and commentary on the Memorandum of Understanding between
         Tungavik Federation of Nunavut and the Fort Churchill Band and the
         Northlands Band (both of Manitoba) on hunting, trapping and fishing in the
         overlap area of the border between the Northwest Territories and Manitoba.

4-191   Memorandum of Understanding Between Tungavik Federation of Nunavut
         (TFN) and the Fort Churchill Band and the Northlands Band. (1985,
         October). Thompson, Man.: Fort Churchill/Northlands Draft.

         Draft of proposed agreement between Inuit of Nunavut and Indians of
         northern Manitoba on land use and treaty rights in the southern Keewatin,
         Northwest Territories.

4-192   Memorandum of Understanding Between Tungavik Federation of Nunavut
         (TFN) and the Fort Churchill Band and the Northlands Band, July 11, 1986.
         (1986). Thompson, Man.: TFN and the Fort Churchill and Northlands
         Bands.

         Text of an agreement between Inuit of Nunavut and Indians of northern
         Manitoba on land use and treaty rights in the southern Keewatin, Northwest
         Territories.

4-193   Memorandum of Understanding Between Tungavik Federation of Nunavut
         (TFN) and the Fort Churchill Band and the Northlands Band: TFN Draft
         December 18, 1985. (1985). Thompson, Man.: Tungavik Federation of
         Nunavut and the Churchill and Northlands Bands.

         Draft of proposed agreement between Inuit of Nunavut and Indians of
         northern Manitoba on land use and treaty rights in the southern Keewatin,
         Northwest Territories.

4-194   Memorandum of Understanding Regarding Devolution and Constitutional
         Development in the Northwest Territories. (1986). Yellowknife, N.W.T.:
         Government of the N.W.T.

         Draft of understanding between the territorial government and five native
         organizations in the Northwest Territories on the manner and sequence of
         devolution of powers, with the definition of a Nunavut/Denendeh boundary
         being a priority.

4-195   Merritt, J. (1993, March). Nunavut: Preparing for Self-Government. Northern
         Perspectives, 21(1), 3-9.

         Outlines some of the reasons why a small number of Inuit in the Eastern
         Canadian Arctic were able to successfully negotiate creation of a Nunavut
         Territory. Includes map of Nunavut and the New Western Territory, draft
         of Article 4 of the Nunavut Agreement, and reprint of the Nunavut Political
         Accord.

4-196   Merritt, J. (1993, September). Nunavut Inuit Organizations and the Challenges
         of a Post-Land Claims World. Northern Perspectives, 21(3), 12-14.

         Discussion of the responsibilities and challenges facing Inuit organizations,
         such as the Nunavut Tungavik and the Nunavut Trust, after the signing of
         the Nunavut Agreement.

4-197   Milortuk, D. (1987). [Letter to W. McKnight]. Ottawa, Ont.: Nunavut Land
         Claims Office.

         Letter from the President of the Tungavik Federation of Nunavut (TFN) to
         the Minister of Indian Affairs and Northern Development, summarizing the
         main features of negotiation and settlement of the Inuit Comprehensive
         Land Claim, and outlining the major focus on economic self-sufficiency in
         the forthcoming Economic Resources Package.

4-198   Milortuk, D. (1986, November). Petroleum Resources Act Prejudices Claims.
         Nunavut, 5(11), 6.

         Summary of problems caused by Bill C-5, the Canada Petroleum Resources
         Bill, for settlement of claims in Nunavut.

4-199   Milortuk, D. (1986, April). TFN Presentation to the ITC Board April 1986:
         Draft. Ottawa, Ont.: Tungavik Federation of Nunavut.

         Draft of speech to the Board of Inuit Tapirisat of Canada, by the chairman
         to the Tungavik Federation of Nunavut, discussing progress to date on the
         Nunavut claim.

4-200   Molloy, T. (1993, September). Negotiating the Nunavut Agreement: A View
         From the Government's Side. Northern Perspectives, 21(3), 9-11.

         Account of the Federal Government's role and activities in negotiating the
         Nunavut Agreement, by the Chief Negotiator on the landclaim from 1982-
         1993.

4-201   Molloy, T. (1991). Purpose of Nunavut Land Claim Agreement. Ottawa, Ont.:
         Indian and Northern Affairs Canada.

         Brief statement by the chief government negotiator on the basis of, and need
         for a landclaim agreement for the Inuit of Nunavut (eastern part of the
         Northwest Territories).

4-202   Morrison, N. R. (1986, January). TFN Participates in Northern Land Use
         Planning. Nunavut, 5(1), 5.

         Announcement of the Northern Land Use Planning Program, which will
         prepare for the formation of the Nunavut Planning Commission, and of land
         use planning for the Lancaster Sound region.

4-203   Moving Forward to 1999. (1993). Yellowknife, N.W.T.: Northwest Territories
         Legislative Assembly.

         Information package used at the Strategic Planning Workshop held by the
         Caucus of the Legislative Assembly of the Northwest Territories in Fort
         Providence, N.W.T., April 4-6, 1993. The documents summarize
         approaches to political, constitutional, economic and financial change in the
         Northwest Territories, as the Nunavut implementation process occurs.

4-204   Negotiating Schedule. (1988, February). Nunavut, 7(2), 5.

         Chart of negotiating schedule for settlement of the Nunavut Agreement:
         announcement of an Agreement-in-Principle on marine areas and a
         membership chart of the board of the Tungavik Federation of Nunavut
         (TFN).

4-205   Negotiations on "Impact" are Unsuccessful. (1985, March). Nunavut, 4(2), 5.

         Account of a meeting held in Calgary March 18-22, 1985, at which the
         Tungavik Federation of Nunavut and the Federal Government attempted to
         reach agreement on the role and functions of the NIRB (Nunavut Impact
         Review Board).

4-206   Negotiators Deal With "Alienation": Inuit Land Will be Protected From Sale to Third Parties. (1989, September). Nunavut, 8(3), 4-9.

Discussion of highlights of the Agreement-in-Principle concerning registration, alienation and boundaries of Inuit settlement lands in the Nunavut area; DIOS (Designated Inuit Organizations); Marine Boundary Provisions, East Baffin Coast; Hunter Income Support Program; the Economic Package, and General Provisions.

4-207   Negotiators Discuss Management of Water Use. (1984, December). Nunavut, 3(10), 1-2.

Summary of negotiations on inland water use and resources in Nunavut.

4-208   Negotiators Discuss "Phased Implementation". (1984, October). Nunavut Newsletter, 3(8), 3-4.

Article urging phased implementation of parts of the Nunavut landclaim settlement, before signing of the final agreement.

4-209   Negotiators Tackle Tougher Topics. (1984, April). Nunavut Newsletter, 3(2), 2.

Discussion of progress on proposed provisions in the Nunavut landclaims settlement, on equity participation (oil, gas and mining companies), special employment, and Inuit Impact and Benefit Agreements (IIBAs).

4-210   "Never Forget Your Language". (1988, June). Nunavut, 7(5), 2-3.

Discussion of the importance of language rights in a landclaim settlement in Nunavut.

4-211   New Mandate Must Address Inuit Concerns: Tungavik Federation of Nunavut Waits to See Where the Foot Will Fall. (1987, May). Nunavut, 6(5), 2-4.

Decision of TFN position on the new Federal Government policy on landclaims as it relates to Nunavut, the offshore, wildlife harvesting, and other issues.

4-212   The New Nunavut Government: Some Basic Questions and Answers. (1992, March). Nunavut, 11(2), 21-22.

Summary of the structure, purpose and functions of the proposed government for the new jurisdiction of Nunavut.

4-213   New Perspectives Emerge at Nunavut Workshop. (1991, January). Members' Update: Supplement to Arctic Circle, 1(4), 2.

Brief account of a workshop "Nunavut: Nation Building in Canada's North", held by the Canadian Arctic Resources Committee (CARC) in cooperation with the Tungavik Federation of Nunavut (TFN).

4-214   News Release. (1987). Ottawa, Ont.: Tungavik Federation of Nunavut.

Statement containing Inuit ratification of the May 9, 1986 landclaims overlap and boundary agreement and TFN's approval of the boundary and constitutional agreement for division of the Northwest Territories reached by the Nunavut and Western Constitutional Forums. As a result TFN cannot re-negotiate the overlap agreement as proposed by the Dene/Metis Negotiating Secretariat on February 25, 1987. (Includes map of the areas in question).

4-215   Nicol, D. (1984, March). Three New Documents Ensure Rights. Nunavut Newsletter, 3-4.

Outline of the Agreements-in-Principle on territorial parks, conservation areas, and ethnographic and archival materials, to be incorporated into an agreement on land and resources in Nunavut.

4-216   No Value to Inuit. (1983, April). Nunavut Newsletter, 6.

Commentary on economic aspects of the Nunavut negotiations including cash compensation and future rights to royalties.

4-217   Northwest Territories. Commission for Constitutional Development (1992). Interim Report. Yellowknife, N.W.T.: The Commission.

Tabled document no. 21-12(2) tabled on March 9, 1992. Report of hearings held in communities of the western Northwest Territories by the Commission for Constitutional Development, concerning the creation of the New Western Territory (Denendeh or Nahendeh) after the formation of Nunavut. Includes commentary on a new constitution, aboriginal and treaty rights, schedule of hearings and terms of reference.

4-218   Northwest Territories Government (1984). Municipal Lands Provisions of an Agreement-in-Principle: January 21, 1984. Ottawa, Ont.: s.n.

Copy of part 3 of an Agreement-in-Principle on municipal lands, between the Federal Government of Canada and the Tungavik Federation of Nunavut, part of a comprehensive claim on Nunavut.

4-219   Northwest Territories Legislative Assembly Caucus (1993). Second Strategic Planning Workshop, Cambridge Bay October 1993. Yellowknife, N.W.T.: Northwest Territories Legislative Assembly.

Information package on the operation of consensus governments and division (into Nunavut and Denendeh) in the Northwest Territories, for caucus members who may make recommendations on these issues to the Legislative Assembly.

4-220   Northwest Territories. Legislative Assembly. Special Committee on Constitutional Reform (1991). Interim Report on the Activities of the Special Committee. Yellowknife, N.W.T.: The Committee.

Committee report no. 07-12(2) tabled on March 12, 1992. This collection of documents covers the reports, presentations and meetings of the Northwest Territories Special Committee on Constitutional Reform, including the territorial position on the Canadian constitution, aboriginal landclaims and the formation of Nunavut.

4-221   Northwest Territories. Legislative Assembly. Special Committee on the Impact of Division (1981). Report of the Special Committee on the Impact of Division of the Northwest Territories. Yellowknife, N.W.T.: The Committee.

Conclusions relate to four boundary proposals: the Inuit Tapirisat of Canada proposal, the Dene Nation proposal, the 1963 federal government proposal, and the same proposal excluding the High Arctic Islands as a federal preserve.

4-222   Northwest Territories. Office of the Chief Plebiscite Officer (1992). Report of the Chief Plebiscite Officer on the Plebiscite on the Boundary for Division of the Northwest Territories held May 4, 1992. Yellowknife, N.W.T.: Northwest Territories Legislative Assembly.

Tabled document no. 65-12(2) tabled on June 25, 1992. Summary of results, details by plebiscite district and polling division, of the vote taken on the proposed boundary between the eastern (Nunavut) and western (Denendeh) parts of the Northwest Territories.

4-223   Nunavut. (1983). Yellowknife, N.W.T.: Nunavut Constitutional Forum.

Pamphlet which uses question and answer format to describe Nunavut, a proposal for territorial-type government to be established by Inuit beyond treeline in N.W.T.

4-224   Nunavut. (1984). Ottawa, Ont.: Nunavut Land Claims Project, Tungavik Federation of Nunavut.

Periodical publication providing the political activity of native peoples towards the establishment of the proposed Nunavut region. The issues dealt with revolve around the central theme of self-determination through political process: devolution, constitutional development, division, landclaims, natural and wildlife resource management, parks land use policy, environmental policy, historical resource law, and social and economic policy. (Previously called: Nunavut Newsletter, to v.3, no. 8, 1984).

4-225   Nunavut 1999: In the Words of the People. (1993, August). Uphere, 9(4), 12-21.

This survey of opinions of Nunavut and northerners' expectations of the new territory, is based on interviews with residents of all three regions; Baffin, Kitikmeot, and Keewatin.

4-226   Nunavut: A Report on Land Claims From the Tungavik Federation of Nunavut.
        Ottawa, Ont.: The Federation.

        Periodical publication reporting the progress of the TFN's landclaims
        negotiations.

4-227   Nunavut Committee on National Issues. (1989, February 15). Northern
        Decisions, 6(19), 146.

        Establishment of a committee to plan and prepare for the new territory of
        Nunavut, including representatives of the Tungavik Federation of Nunavut,
        Inuit Tapirisat of Canada, and Members of Parliament.

4-228   Nunavut Constitutional Forum (1983). Brief of the Nunavut Constitutional
        Forum to the Royal Commission on the Economic Union and Development
        Prospects for Canada (the Macdonald Commission). Yellowknife, N.W.T.:
        Nunavut Constitutional Forum.

        Brief presented to Royal Commission on Economic Union and
        Development Prospects for Canada by Nunavut Constitutional Forum.
        Outlines main issues in present evolution of Nunavut. Asserts that Inuit
        want reasonable landclaims settlements and a Nunavut territorial
        government.

4-229   Nunavut Constitutional Forum (1983). Building Nunavut: A Discussion Paper
        Containing Proposals for an Arctic Constitution . Yellowknife, N.W.T.:
        Nunavut Constitutional Forum.

        Discusses the proposals and conditions included in the Nunavut
        constitution, concerning landclaims, self-government, and socio-economic
        issues.

4-230   Nunavut Constitution: Rights to Lands and Resources. (1983, May). Nunavut
        Newsletter, 6-7.

        Outline of the rights to lands and resources to be included in the proposed
        Nunavut Constitution, including commissioners' lands, oil and gas revenues,
        minerals, landclaims, government, boundaries, a bill of rights, a legislative
        assembly, and language.

4-231   Nunavut Constitutional Forum. (1984, September 30). Northern Decisions,
        2(11), 70.

        Report of establishment of principles to guide ongoing discussions on the
        role and responsibilities of regional bodies in Nunavut, at a meeting in
        Cambridge Bay (8-9 Sept. 1984) between the Nunavut Constitutional
        Forum and regional council representatives.

4-232   Nunavut Constitutional Forum. (1985, March 15). Northern Decisions, 2(21),
        148.

        Note on funding for the Nunavut Constitutional Forum for the fiscal year
        1984-1985.

4-233   Nunavut Constitutional Forum Workshop, 1984, Cambridge Bay. (1984).
         <u>Minutes: Nunavut Constitutional Forum Workshop With Regional
         Councils</u>. Cambridge Bay, N.W.T., 1984, September 9. Ottawa, Ont.:
         Nunavut Constitutional Forum.

         Minutes of workshop devoted to trying to ascertain a local/
         regional/Territorial division of governmental power within Nunavut.

4-234   Nunavut Government in Five Years? (1983, March). <u>Nunavut Newsletter</u>, 4-5.

         Report by the chairman of the NCF (Nunavut Constitutional Forum) on the
         possibility of a Nunavut Government within five years.

4-235   <u>The Nunavut Land Claim Agreement in Plain Language</u>. (1992). Ottawa, Ont.:
         Tungavik Federation of Nunavut.

         Plain English version, for the general public, of the Agreement between the
         Inuit of the Nunavut Settlement Area (eastern part of the Northwest
         Territories) and the Government of Canada, prepared for a ratification vote
         by the Inuit as represented by the Tungavik Federation of Nunavut (TFN).
         Terms cover political development, wildlife, compensation, outpost camps,
         land and resource management and planning, water rights, marine areas,
         landfast ice zone, land title and access, taxation, government employment
         and contracts, resource royalties, capital transfer, the Inuit Heritage Trust,
         The Nunavut Trust, the Nunavut Social Development Council, archaeology,
         enrollment and ratification process, implementation and arbitration.

4-236   Nunavut Land Claims Change. (1988, February). <u>ITC News</u>, 10.

         Brief account of changes in ITC (Inuit Tapirisat of Canada) policy on the
         Nunavut landclaims project as a result of a landclaims workshop in Rankin
         Inlet.

4-237   Nunavut Leaders Meeting (1994: Rankin Inlet, N.W.T.) (1994). <u>Declaration
         and Statements From the Meeting</u>. Yellowknife, N.W.T.: Legislative
         Assembly of the Northwest Territories.

         Statements of position on various aspects of Nunavut (education,
         devolution of powers, conduct of leaders, Quebec claims to territory) by
         principal members of Inuit organizations, at a meeting held January 14-17
         1994.

4-238   Nunavut Leaders' Summit. (1992, March). <u>Members' Update: Supplement to
         Arctic Circle</u>, 2(5), 2.

         Summary of meeting in Iqaluit, N.W.T. in January 1992, at which Inuit
         leaders agreed on various aspects of Nunavut, including start-up date of
         1999, the plebiscite for a new boundary, and a transition and implementation
         commission.

4-239   Nunavut Means "Our Land". (1993, December). <u>Pemmican Journal</u>, 14-16.

Summary of progress to date on the creation of Nunavut, with a brief chronology, and outline of the agreement on wildlife, and description of the Inuit position on landclaims.

4-240   Nunavut Negotiations. (1985, November). <u>Nunasi Report</u>, 26(6), 7.

Response by Paul Sammurtok, project director of the Tungavik Federation of Nunavut, to federal government moves to place deadlines on landclaims negotiations, and comment on the MacDonald Commission Report.

4-241   Nunavut Negotiators Prepare for New Phase. (1985, July). <u>Nunavut</u>, 4(5), 2.

Summary of activities by the Tungavik Federation of Nunavut on land identification, the creation of a Nunavut Impact Review Board (NIRB) and the social provisions of a Nunavut settlement.

4-242   <u>Nunavut, Our Land, Our People</u>. (1993). s.l.: Nunavut Tungavik Incorporated.

Summary of the basic information and statistics on the Inuit territory of Nunavut, to be implemented by 1999.

4-243   <u>Nunavut Political Accord</u>. (1992). Yellowknife, N.W.T.: Government of the Northwest Territories.

Tabled document no. 1-12(3) tabled on November 17, 1992. Text of the Accord between the Tungavik Federation of Nunavut, the Government of Canada and the Government of the Northwest Territories on the transition process and timetable for the creation of Nunavut, as well as financing, administrative capacity of the government and training and human resources planning. Includes definition of the western boundary.

4-244   Nunavut Revisited: Nation Building in Canada's North. (1990). <u>Northern Perspectives</u>, 18(4), 1-28.

Proceedings of conference organized by Canadian Arctic Resources Committee (CARC) and Tungavik Federation of Nunavut (TFN), on progress towards creation of the new Inuit territory.

4-245   Nunavut: Vision or Illusion? (1990, March). <u>Canadian Parliamentary Review</u>, 13, 6-10.

Edited transcript of a debate on October 31, 1989 in the 11th Legislative Assembly of the Northwest Territories, on a motion introduced by Peter Ernerk to affirm support for creation of a Nunavut territory.

4-246   Nunavut Wildlife Management Agreement Re-Initialed. (1986, June). <u>Nunavut</u>, 5(6), 2

Re-signing, with amendments, of the Nunavut Wildlife Management Agreement, which includes the Nunavut Wildlife Management Board with powers of decision making.

4-247   Nunavut-Closer To Reality. (1992, June). <u>Transition</u>, 5(6), 1,7.

Commentary on the results of the May 4, 1992 plebiscite on the proposed boundary between Nunavut and the rest of the Northwest Territories.

4-248   Offshore Waters and Islands Used by Inuit in Both Nunavut and Quebec. (1988, April). <u>Nunavut</u>, 7(4), 6.

Outline of the Memorandum of Understanding (MOU) between the Tungavik Federation of Nunavut, and Makivik, regarding Offshore Boundaries and Areas of Overlapping Use, dealing with hunting by Inuit of Nunavut and northern Quebec in Hudson Bay, Hudson Strait, James Bay, and Ungava Bay.

4-249   Okalik, L. (1993, September). Capital of Nunavut Territory: Time is Nearer to Designate the Capital of NT. <u>Nunavut</u>, 12(5), 12,14.

Discussion of possible choices for the capital of Nunavut.

4-250   Okalik, L. (1993, September). Letter of Invitation to Nunavut Residents: Participation in the Growth of Canada. <u>Nunavut</u>, 12(5), 1.

Editorial urging Inuit in all regions to become informed and participate in implementation of the Nunavut Land Claims Agreement.

4-251   Okalik, L. (1993, September). NTI Board Meeting in Baker Lake, NWT. <u>Nunavut</u>, 12(5), 3, 5.

Account of the meeting of the Board of Nunavut Tungavik Incorporated and a workshop held to inform Baker Lake residents of details of funding and programs to be delivered under the Nunavut Agreement.

4-252   Okalik, L. (1991, July). Agreement on Lake Harbour Land Quantum. <u>Nunavut</u>, 10(2), 9-10.

Account of negotiations for Inuit lands at Lake Harbour, N.W.T., during December 1990, by the Community Land Identification Negotiating Team (CLINT), the Tungavik Federation of Nunavut and the Federal Government of Canada.

4-253   Okalik, L. (1993, July). Coppermine Celebrations, July 8-11, 1993. <u>Nunavut</u>, 12(4), 21, 23.

Description of the community of Coppermine, NWT on the occasion of the visit by the Minister of Indian and Northern Affairs, to declare Royal Assent to the Nunavut Agreement and the Nunavut Act. (Translated from English to Inuktitut: Simona Arnatsiaq-Barnes.)

4-254   Okalik, L. (1993, May). Functions of the Nunavut Tungavik Inc. Nunavut, 12(3), 1-4.

Description of the structure and functions of the Nunavut Tungavik Inc., the body created to implement the provisions of the Nunavut Final Agreement. Includes organizational chart.

4-255   Okalik, L. (1992, November). Inuit Ratify the Nunavut Agreement. Nunavut, 11(6), 6-8.

Results of the ratification of the Nunavut Agreement, November 1992, including text of the ballot question.

4-256   Okalik, L. (1992, November). Nunavut Political Accord Signed in Iqaluit, N.W.T.: October 30, 1992 - Inuksuk High School. Nunavut, 11(6), 22.

Account of the signing of the Nunavut Political Accord on October 30, 1992, Iqaluit, Northwest Territories.

4-257   Okalik, L. (1993, July). Nunavut Tungavik Inc. Board Meeting Coppermine, NWT July 10-11, 1993. Nunavut, 12(4), 24.

Summary of resolutions at the Nunavut Tungavik Inc. (NTI) meeting, including funding, costs of different proposed locations for a capital of Nunavut, and mode of operation.

4-258   Okalik, L. (1993, July). Poetry on Signing of the Nunavut Agreement. Nunavut, 12(4), 6-14.

Prose poem/narrative description of the signing of the Nunavut Agreement in Iqaluit, NWT, May 25, 1993.

4-259   Okalik, L. (1991, July). Procedures Taken During Negotiations. Nunavut, 10(2), 20.

Summary of procedures used in Pangnirtung in selecting Inuit lands, by the Community Land Identification Negotiating Teams (CLINT), Tungavik Federation of Nunavut and the Federal Government of Canada, in 1990.

4-260   Okalik, L. (1991, October). Ratification Committee Working on Final Agreement Vote. Nunavut, 10(4), 10.

Explanation of how the ratification vote by Inuit on the Nunavut Land Claim Final Agreement, will be organized.

4-261 Okalik, L. (1992, May). Ratification Committee: Who, Where and What Do They Do? And Why? Nunavut, 11(3), 6-8.

Account of the functions, membership and timetable of the Ratification Committee established to ensure Inuit understand the landclaim agreement of December 1991.

4-262 Okalik, L. (1993, July). Special General Meeting Tungavik Assembly Coppermine, NWT, July 12-13, 1993. Nunavut, 12(4), 26- 28.

Summary of the proceedings of the meeting on matters arising from the Nunavut Land Claim Agreement.

4-263 Okalik, L. (1991, July). What is Land Selection? Nunavut, 10(2), 15-16.

Description of the process of selection of Inuit lands in Nunavut, with definitions of terminology, by the Community Land Identification Negotiating Teams (CLINT), Tungavik Federation of Nunavut and the Federal Government of Canada.

4-264 Okalik, L. (1993, May). Who is Involved in Implementing the Nunavut Land Claim Final Agreement? Nunavut, 12(3), 6.

Explanation of the membership and committees of the Nunavut Tunngavik Inc., the corporation created on April 1, 1993 to implement the Nunavut Final Agreement until the Government and Territory are created in 1999.

4-265 Okalik, P. (1991, December). Paul Okalik Talks About the Path to Final Agreement: What's to be Expected. Nunavut, 10(1), 11-12.

Outline of work to be done between the signing of the Agreement-in-Principle on Nunavut (April 30, 1990) and a Final Agreement and ratification.

4-266 Okalik, P. (1993, March). NWMB and Inuit Hunting Rights. Nunavut, 12(2), 7-9.

Summary of the provisions of the Nunavut Land Claims Agreement regarding wildlife and the Nunavut Wildlife Management Board in relation to traditional hunting activities.

4-267 Outline of TFN Claim Settlement Package. (1988, September). Building Blocks, (9), 5.

Chart of negotiated and outstanding components to date of the Tungavik Federation of Nunavut Claim.

4-268 Outpost Camp Agreement. (1983, July). Nunavut Newsletter, 12.

Outline of the provisions of the Outpost Camp Agreement, for Inuit residents of the proposed territory of Nunavut.

4-269   <u>Overlap Agreement Between the Dene/Metis and the Tungavik Federation of Nunavut May 9, 1986</u>. (1986). Yellowknife, N.W.T.: Dene/Metis Negotiator and the Tungavik Federation of Nunavut.

Text of the agreement on the boundary between the Dene/Metis and Nunavut claims in the Northwest Territories (to be ratified in Iqaluit, 1987).

4-270   <u>Overlapping Claims in Northwest Territories</u>. (1983). Communique, 1-8325. Ottawa, Ont.: Indian and Northern Affairs Canada.

Announcement of establishment of a dual process to help resolve the overlap of lands claimed by three native groups (Dene, Metis, Inuit) in the Northwest Territories, with the appointment of W. C. Wonders as a fact-finder and R. W. Hornal as facilitator in bringing the groups together. Claims involved are Committee for Original Peoples' Entitlement (COPE); Dene/Metis in the Mackenzie Valley; and Nunavut (Tungavik Federation of Nunavut).

4-271   Paniaq, M. (1989, December). TFN Seeks Arbitration in Shared Boundary Debate. <u>Nunavut</u>, 8(1), 12.

Account of negotiations between Inuit, Dene and Metis of the Northwest Territories, Manitoba and Saskatchewan on the proposed boundary of Nunavut.

4-272   Paniaq, M. (1990, December). Thinking Ahead: What is Land Use Planning? <u>Nunavut</u>, 9(1), 9-10.

Discussion of the meaning and significance of land use planning in Nunavut, and details of the Nunavut Planning Commission established in 1989.

4-273   Park Reserve Will Protect Fragile Environment. (1986, October). <u>Nunavut</u>, 5(10), 10.

Announcement of the establishment of the Ellesmere Island National Park Reserve, and its relation to the Nunavut land claim settlement.

4-274   Parker, J. H. (1991). <u>The Boundary Between Comprehensive Claim Settlement Areas of the Inuit and Dene/Metis of the Northwest Territories: a Report to the Honourable Tom Siddon, Minister of Indian Affairs and Northern Development</u>. Ottawa, Ont.: Department of Indian Affairs and Northern Development.

Recommendations on the location of the land boundary between the proposed territory of Nunavut and the balance of the Northwest Territories, further to the fact-finding review by Magnus Gunther.

4-275   <u>Partners for the Future: a Selection of Papers Related to Constitutional Development in the Western Northwest Territories</u>. (1984). s.l.: Western Constitutional Forum.

Includes: Address to the Standing Committee on Indian Affairs by the Western Constitutional Forum: ways to interface aboriginal self-government with public government in the western N.W.T.: the relevance of consociation: Inuvialuit self-government: municipal government and land within municipal boundaries: land rights for a western territory: official status for languages in Canada.

4-276 Patrick, A. R. (1986). <u>Submission to the Advisory Commission on the Development of Government in the Northwest Territories</u>. Edmonton, Alta.: Department of Industry and Development.

Submission to the Carrothers Commission suggesting that the Yukon Territory and the Mackenzie Basin of the N.W.T should be incorporated into the western provinces.

4-277 Patterson, D. (1987). <u>Creating a Better Tomorrow: Aboriginal Claims in the Northwest Territories</u>. Yellowknife, N.W.T.: Aboriginal Rights and Constitutional Development Secretariat, N.W.T.

Background information to give an understanding of what landclaims are all about, who is involved in the process of negotiating a settlement and how the interests of different groups are represented.

4-278 Patterson, D. (1984). <u>Notes for Statement by the Honourable Dennis Patterson, Minister for Aboriginal Rights and Constitutional Development to the 10th Legislative Assembly Concerning the Negotiations Towards the Settlement of the TFN Aboriginal Claim</u>. Yellowknife, N.W.T.: The Government.

Summary of the position of the Federal Government of Canada on settlement of a comprehensive land claim involving municipal lands and the Tungavik Federation of Nunavut.

4-279 Phone for Answers. (1985, May). <u>Nunavut</u>, 4(3), 7.

Announcement of visits to communities by the Tungavik Federation of Nunavut's Community Liaison Workers, to discuss provisions for land title and outpost camps.

4-280 The Plebiscite Question: What Are We Being Asked? (1992, March). <u>Nunavut</u>, 11(2), 14-15.

Explanation of the question to be settled in the plebiscite of May 4, 1992, on the boundary between Nunavut and the rest of the Northwest Territories, with chart of dates of implementation to 2010.

4-281 Polar Sea Spurs Public Debate. (1985, November). <u>Nunavut</u>, 4(6), 10.

Summary of protests by the Tungavik Federation of Nunavut against the voyage of the United States icebreaker "Polar Sea" through the Arctic archipelago in a challenge to Canadian sovereignty.

4-282   Policies Are Inconsistent, Says TFN. (1987, June). Nunavut, 6(5), 6.

Summary of Inuit concerns about the Federal Government's Northern Mineral Policy for increased exploration and mining.

4-283   A Policy in Transition. (1987, January). Northern Perspectives, 15(1), 8-11.

Discussion of documents containing policy statements on native landclaims: "In All Fairness (1981): "Living Treaties: Lasting Agreements, 1985" and the "Policy Statement of the Minister of Indian Affairs and Northern Development (Bill McKnight) in December 1986". The text compares some of the key elements of the 1981 and 1986 policies with the proposals for change contained in the 1985 task force report.

4-284   Preparing for the Settlement: A Training Proposal Submitted by the Tungavik Federation of Nunavut to the Canada Employment and Immigration Commission. (Revised) (1984). Ottawa, Ont.: Tungavik Federation of Nunavut.

Proposal for a ten-month training program designed to equip ten Inuit with knowledge and skills needed to qualify for positions as Community Liaison Workers with the Tungavik Federation of Nunavut until a final agreement is reached on the Nunavut claim.

4-285   Progress in Negotiation of Eastern and Central Arctic Claim. (1983). Communique, 1-8324. Ottawa, Ont.: Indian and Northern Affairs Canada.

Announcement by chief negotiator Tom Molloy that the parties negotiating the Tungavik Federation of Nunavut (TFN) landclaim have reached agreement on provisions for conservation areas.

4-286   Progress in Winnipeg. (1983, January). Nunavut Newsletter, 2.

Report on negotiations on the Wildlife Agreement-in-Principle and the target date of 1984 for the Land and Resources Agreement.

4-287   Provisions Ensure More Government Jobs for Inuit. (1984, June). Nunavut Newsletter, 3(4), 4-5.

Outline of the scope of the Agreement on Provisions for Public Sector Inuit Employment in Nunavut negotiated by the Tungavik Federation of Nunavut and the Federal Government of Canada, as part of the Nunavut landclaim.

4-288   Provisions For Outpost Camps. (1983). Ottawa, Ont.: s.n.

Draft of the section of the Nunavut Agreement affecting outpost camps for Inuit hunters, including terms of title and occupancy.

4-289   Provisions For Public Sector Inuit Employment in Nunavut. (1984). Ottawa, Ont.: Tungavik Federation of Nunavut.

Draft of clauses of the Nunavut Agreement as they would relate to employment, training and pre-employment training of Inuit in government positions in the Nunavut claim area.

4-290   Provisions Give Power to Local Government. (1984, March). Nunavut Newsletter, 1-2.

Outline of the provisions of the Agreement-in-Principle on Municipal Lands in Nunavut.

4-291   Provisions of an Agreement in Principle on Marine Areas. (1985). Ottawa, Ont.: Tungavik Federation of Nunavut.

Outline of clauses for an Agreement-in-Principle in the Nunavut claim area, on marine (offshore) areas with comments on definition, Inuit use of the "fast ice zone" and regulation of such an area.

4-292   Provisions of an Agreement-in-Principle on Marine Areas: TFN Position. (1986). Ottawa, Ont.: Tungavik Federation of Nunavut.

Terms of an Agreement-in-Principle on marine (offshore) areas in the Nunavut claim area, as proposed by the Tungavik Federation of Nunavut, including a Nunavut Marine Council.

4-293   Provisions Will Protect Nunavut's Water. (1985, January). Nunavut, 4(1), 2-5.

Outlines provisions for water use and disposition and the Northern Inland Waters Act, with summary of role and functions of the Nunavut Water Board.

4-294   Provisions Will Protect Rights and Wildlife. (1986, July). Nunavut, 5(7), 2.

Commentary on the provisions of the Agreement-in-Principle on wildlife in Nunavut.

4-295   Purich, D. J. (1992). The Inuit and Their Land: the Story of Nunavut. Toronto, Ont.: J. Lorimer.

This book tells the story of the Inuit, their land, and their long struggle for self-government. It explores the difficulties that must be overcome before the new territory (Nunavut, the eastern part of the present Northwest Territories) can become a reality and discusses the pros and cons of a landclaim settlement.

4-296   Qanatsiaq, J. (1985, July). Inuit will get Protection for Hunting Camps. Nunavut, 4(5), 5.

Summary of Agreement-in-Principle on provisions for outpost camps in Nunavut.

4-297   Qanatsiaq, J. (1985, June). Let's Take a Look at Land Ownership. Nunavut, 4(4), 6-7.

Commentary on land ownership in Nunavut by a Community Liaison Worker with the Tungavik Federation of Nunavut.

4-298   Quassa, P. (1991, December). Signing of the Nunavut Land Claim Agreement-in-Principle Speech, Igloolik, April 30, 1990 by Paul Quassa, TFN President and Chief Negotiator. Nunavut, 10(1), 2-4.

Speech made by the President and Chief Negotiator for the Tungavik Federation of Nunavut, Paul Quassa, at the signing of the Nunavut Agreement-in-Principle at Igloolik, N.W.T. on April 30, 1990, with a description and photographs of the ceremony.

4-299   Quassa, P. (1993, July). The Signing of the Final Agreement: Speech Notes For Paul Quassa, President of Nunavut Tungavik Inc. May 25, 1993, Iqaluit, NWT. Nunavut, 12(4), 3, 5.

Commentary on the occasion of the signing of the Nunavut Agreement.

4-300   The Ratification Poster. (1992, May). Nunavut, 11(3), 10-11.

Copy of the poster announcing the date for the vote on ratification of the Nunavut Land Claim Agreement (November 3-5, 1992).

4-301   Recent Developments With Respect to the Creation of a Nunavut Territory. (1991, July). Nunavut, 10(2), 8.

Summary of Article 4 of the Tungavik Federation of Nunavut Agreement-in-Principle (1990) dealing with timetable and funding for Nunavut.

4-302   Regional Land Quantums: Inuit Land Square Miles. (1991, July). Nunavut, 10(2), 12.

Summary, with tables, of Inuit lands retained by thirteen Nunavut communities under the Agreement-in-Principle of 1990.

4-303   Regions Reflect Uniqueness of Land. (1988, April). Nunavut, 7(4), 5.

Explanation of how Inuit-owned land will be defined and identified for each community in Nunavut, by Community Land Identification Negotiating Teams (CLINT) who will negotiate both the quantum and the boundaries, with a guarantee of at least 75% of the areas first identified as "Areas of Interest". Includes listing of communities of each of the six regions, and names of coordinators.

4-304   Re-Organization Will Save Nunasi Money. (1986, October). Nunavut, 5(10), 2.

Explanation of the re-organization of Nunasi, the business development organization for all Inuit in the Tungavik Federation of Nunavut claims area.

4-305   Report on the Nature and Cost of the Transition to Nunavut. (1984, October).
s.l.: DPA Group for Indian and Northern Affairs Canada.

Report commissioned by the Federal Department of Indian and Northern
Affairs to focus on the timing, activities, and costs required to effect the
transition from the status quo to the full operation of Nunavut as a political
and legal entity within Canada.

4-306   A Review of the Boundary and Overlap Negotiations Between the Tungavik
Federation of Nunavut and the Dene/Metis Negotiations Secretariat. (1989).
Ottawa, Ont.: Tungavik Federation of Nunavut.

Summary of the progress of talks on the boundary overlap areas of the
Nunavut and Dene/Metis claims in the Northwest Territories, including the
Iqaluit Agreement of 1987, subsequent actions and federal policy on the
issue.

4-307   Riewe, R. (1991). Inuit Land Use Studies and the Native Claims Process. In K.
Abel, & J. Friesen (Editors), Aboriginal Resource Use in Canada: Historical
and Legal Aspects. Manitoba Studies in Native History 6, (pp. 287-299).
Winnipeg, Man.: University of Manitoba Press.

Summary of the methodology and goals of the "Inuit Land Use and
Occupancy Project" and the "Nunavut Atlas" in relation to the Tungavik
Federation of Nunavut (TFN) Land Claim on behalf of the Inuit of the
eastern Arctic.

4-308   Riewe, R. (1992). Inuit Land Use and Occupancy in the Southern Keewatin,
N.W.T. Edmonton, Alta.: Canadian Circumpolar Institute.

This report briefly summarizes the published reports on Inuit land in
Nunavut focusing on the southern Keewatin, Northwest Territories, in areas
also claimed by Dene and Metis groups from Manitoba and Saskatchewan
as traditional areas for hunting. The mapped information for these areas is
re-evaluated.

4-309   Riewe, R. (1986). Inuit Use and Concerns of the Overlap Zone Between Great
Bear and Pellet Lakes. Edmonton, Alta.: Rick Riewe.

This survey of land use by Inuit hunters and trappers in a boundary overlap
area of the Northwest Territories (claimed by both Inuit and Dene as part of
landclaim settlements) focuses on data from Coppermine area residents.

4-310   Riewe, R. (1991). Inuit Use of the Sea Ice. Arctic and Alpine Research, 23(1),
3-10.

Presents archaeological and present data on sea ice use. Includes brief
analyses of hunting ranges over sea ice by Arviat (Keewatin, N.W.T.) and
Grise Fiord (Ellesmere Island, N.W.T.) communities, Inuit sea ice
terminology, and sovereignty and landclaims implications.

4-311   Riewe, R. (1988). Land Use Mapping and Regional Variations Within Nunavut. In R. Riewe, P. Adams, & F. Duerden (Editors), <u>Polar Science, Technology and Information. Tenth Anniversary Conference of ACUNS, Ryerson Polytechnic Institute May 1-2, 1987</u>, (pp. 80-85). Ottawa, Ont.: Association of Canadian Universities For Northern Studies.

Report by the coordinator of the Land Identification Project on mapping activities intended to assist Inuit with identification of lands to be retained after settlement of landclaims negotiations for Nunavut.

4-312   Riewe, R. (1986). <u>L.I.P. Progress Report March - May 1986</u>. Eskimo Point, N.W.T.: Land Identification Project.

Summary of work to date on the Land Identification Project for the Tungavik Federation of Nunavut and discussion of principles and procedures for work with the Inuit communities in selecting land.

4-313   Riewe, R. (1992). <u>Nunavut Atlas</u>. Circumpolar Research Series, 2. Edmonton, Alta.: Canadian Circumpolar Institute and The Tungavik Federation of Nunavut.

This atlas illustrates and describes the geographical extent of Inuit land use in the Nunavut Agreement area (eastern Northwest Territories) in terms of intensity of use (high, medium, low) and of type of wildlife (caribou calving grounds, waterfowl nesting ranges and migration routes of animals harvested), based on data collected from hunters and elders in the communities.

4-314   Riewe, R. (1985). <u>Report on the Activities and Plans of the Land Identification Project Coordinator</u>. Ottawa, Ont.: Nunavut Land Claims Project.

Budget and workplan for the Coordinator and staff of the Land Identification Project (for the Tungavik Federation of Nunavut), which will identify Inuit lands used by each community in the claim area.

4-315   Riewe, R., Suluk, L., & Brandson, L. (1989). Inuit Land Use and Occupancy in Northern Manitoba. <u>Northern Review</u>, (3-4), 85- 95.

Documents past and present land use by Inuit and their predecessors (Thule, Dorset, and pre-Dorset cultures) as far south as Churchill, Manitoba. Intention is to support Inuit landclaim (Nunavut).

4-316   Robertson, G. (1987, May). Nunavut and the International Arctic. <u>Northern Perspectives</u>, 15(2), 9.

An "Inuit Territory" could play a role in Canada's growing interest in the international arctic. It might underscore "effective occupation", the surest grounds in international law for a claim of sovereignty.

4-317   Robertson, G. (1987). Political Development for the Northern Future. s.l.: s.n.

Argues that provincial status will not be a feasible solution for future political development in the north. Calls for the establishment of Nunavut and full self-government for the remaining territories with special constitutional protections for the cultural security of the aboriginal peoples.

4-318   Saali Peter Writes to John Munro and John Munro Writes Back. (1984, April). Nunavut Newsletter, 3(2), 4-5.

Correspondence between an Inuit of Iqaluit and the Minister of Indian Affairs and Northern Development, on the progress of the Nunavut Land Claim.

4-319   Signing the Nunavut Final Land Claim. (1993, June). Makivik News, (27), 26-31.

Account of the signing of the Final Nunavut Agreement in Iqaluit, Northwest Territories on May 25, 1993. Includes map of Inuit owned lands.

4-320   Sixteen-Year Fight by Claimants Against "Extinguishment" Was Not in Vain. (1989, March). Nunavut, 8(2), 2-3.

Discussion of the position of the Tungavik Federation of Nunavut on extinguishment of aboriginal title as part of the landclaim agreement in negotiation with the Government of Canada.

4-321   Sound Planning Requires Cooperative Approach. (1986, October). Nunavut, 5(10), 11.

Announcement of the formation of the Lancaster Sound Land Use Planning Commission, in accordance with the agreement-in-principle on landuse planning for Nunavut signed in July, 1984.

4-322   Special Report: An Open Letter to the People of the Northwest Territories. (1986, March). Nunavut, 5(3), 5.

Open letter to the people of the Northwest Territories from the Tungavik Federation of Nunavut, explaining the purpose of the Inuit Impact and Benefit Agreement (IIBA).

4-323   Spence, G. (1991, October). Enrollment and Eligibility: Nunavut Appeals Committee Established. Nunavut, 10(4), 16.

Explanation of how Inuit are to enroll as beneficiaries under the Nunavut Final Agreement, and the role of the Nunavut Appeals Committee.

4-324   Stenbaek, M. (1983, February). Nunavut - A New Hope for an Inuit Territory in Canada. The Arctic Policy Review, 13-15.

Discussion of the Federal government support for division of the Northwest Territories (announced November 1982) and the conditions necessary for implementation: support by residents, resolution of landclaims, consensus on boundaries, and re-distribution of powers between three levels of government.

4-325   Suluk, T. (1989). Nunavut: None Of It, Some Of It, All Of It. Ottawa, Ont.: Thomas Suluk.

Report to his constituents in the eastern Arctic, by the Member of Parliament for Nunatsiaq, on recent progress on landclaims and a boundary for division of the Northwest Territories into Nunavut and Denendeh, including a map of the overlap area.

4-326   Summary of the Agreement Between the Inuit of the Nunavut Settlement Area and Her Majesty in Right of Canada. (1992). Yellowknife, N.W.T.: Inuit Ratification Committee.

Summary text (not authoritative) of the Agreement between the Inuit of the Nunavut Settlement Area (eastern part of the Northwest Territories) and the Government of Canada, prepared for a ratification vote by the Inuit as represented by the Tungavik Federation on Nunavut (TFN). Includes legal description of boundaries, and map (for information only). Terms cover political development, wildlife, compensation, outpost camps, land and resource management and planning, water rights, marine areas, landfast ice zone, land title and access, contracts, resource royalties, capital transfer, the Inuit Heritage Trust, the Nunavut Trust, the Nunavut Social Development Council, archaeology, enrollment and ratification process, implementation and arbitration.

4-327   Summary of Wildlife Agreement-in-Principle. (1982, July 15). Nunavut Newsletter, (2), 7-9.

Summary of the intent and provisions of the Wildlife Agreement-in-Principle, initialed in 1981, and the Nunavut Wildlife Management Board.

4-328   Survey Responses Can Help TFN Do a Better Job. (1984, June). Nunavut Newsletter, 3(4), 2-3.

Summary of Inuit concerns about the Nunavut landclaim process.

4-329   Swiderski, A. L. (1989). Development Planning in the Eastern Arctic: The Role of Communities in a Comprehensive Development Strategy. Doctoral Dissertation, York University, North York, Ont.

The role of communities in a comprehensive development strategy in the eastern Arctic is examined from a broad perspective, including the emerging processes and implications of the Nunavut proposal and the Inuit landclaim. Evidence from other existing landclaim settlements is presented to provide pragmatic consideration of the potential for change.

4-330 Task Force on Inuit Management Development (1986). A Strategy for Inuit
       Management Development: The Report of the Task Force on Inuit
       Management Development. Ottawa, Ont.: Inuit Tapirisat of Canada.

       Report from task force initiated by Inuit and territorial government leaders
       to prepare Inuit for management responsibilities in the Baffin, Keewatin, and
       Kitikmeot regions of the Northwest Territories (area called Nunavut).
       Provides a long-range training strategy linked to the unique political and
       economic opportunities of the far North.

4-331 The Task Force Report: TFN Supports Major Policy Recommendations. (1986,
       May). Nunavut, 5(5).

       Commentary on the report of the Federal Government Task Force which
       reviewed "In All Fairness" and wrote the report "Living Treaties, Lasting
       Agreements", which explains what the framework, substance and process of
       any new landclaims agreement should be.

4-332 TFN and Dene/Metis Agree on a Boundary. (1986, June). Nunavut, 5(6), 3.

       Announcement, with map, of preliminary agreement between the Inuit and
       Dene of the Northwest Territories, on a land boundary and overlap zones
       for Nunavut and the western territory.

4-333 TFN and Government Cross Major Hurdle. (1988, April). Nunavut, 7(4), 2.

       Explanation of how Inuit-owned land will be defined and identified for each
       community in Nunavut, by Community Land Identification Negotiating
       Teams (CLINT's) who will negotiate both the quantum and the boundaries,
       with a guarantee of at least 75% of the areas first identified as "Areas of
       Interest". Includes listing of communities of each of the six regions, and
       names of coordinators.

4-334 TFN Changes Its Position: Feds Disappointed. (1983, January). Nunavut
       Newsletter, 3.

       Discussion of the position of the Tungavik Federation of Nunavut on
       impact assessment, both economic and social, for major development
       projects proposed in the North.

4-335 TFN Claim: Claims Update. (1986, September). Building Blocks, (5), 3.

       Report on work in progress on the role of the Nunavut Impact Review
       Board (NIRB) and the offshore component of the Tungavik Federation of
       Nunavut (TFN) claim.

4-336 TFN Claim: Claims Update. (1988, September). Building Blocks, (9), 3.

       Report of progress to date on 26 initialed sub-agreements and a number of
       discussion papers, including the land quantum, taxation, and land and water
       management boards.

4-337   TFN Claim: Negotiations. (1986, August). Building Blocks, (4), 2.

Notice of negotiations in Coppermine in August 1986 and a workshop in Ottawa to study the various environmental regulatory authorities under which governments operate, including the proposed Nunavut Impact and Assessment Review Board.

4-338   TFN Claim: Overview of the Inuit Impact and Benefit Agreements. (1986, July). Building Blocks, (3), 1.

Summary of the contents of the Inuit Impact and Benefit Agreements (IIBA) initialed in Ottawa January 17, 1986.

4-339   TFN Claim Update. (1989, January). Building Blocks, (10), 5.

Report on progress on sub-agreements and discussion papers for the Tungavik Federation of Nunavut claim, including land quantum negotiations for the regions.

4-340   TFN Claim Update. (1989, April). Building Blocks, (11), 4-5.

Report of progress on the Tungavik Federation of Nunavut claim, including agreement on settlement area boundary provisions as they apply to the East Baffin Coast (i.e. concerning land fast ice) and a sub-agreement on designated Inuit organizations.

4-341   TFN, Government Agree on Ratification Process. (1988, July). Nunavut, 7(6), 2.

Announcement of the initialing of: the Ratification Provisions of an Agreement-in-Principle: The Title to Inuit Lands (including ownership and access to carving stone / soap stone deposits): The Wildlife Compensation Agreement (compensation for loss of income, food and property of Inuit caused by development activity in Nunavut).

4-342   TFN, Government Reach Agreement on Eligibility and Enrollment Process. (1987, January). Nunavut, 6(1), 2-3.

Report of settlement of the question of who is eligible to enroll, and how they will enroll, as beneficiaries of Nunavut.

4-343   TFN Needs Answers Now to Crucial Questions. (1987, September). Nunavut, 6(7), 2-10.

Summaries of progress in negotiations on Inuit ownership of land in Nunavut: on natural resource management: on bodies with guaranteed Inuit representation (Nunavut Wildlife Management Board, Nunavut Land Use Planning Commission, Nunavut Impact Review Board, Nunavut Water Board, and Inuit Impact and Benefit Agreements (IIBA's): on the Northern Inland Waters Act, and on the Lancaster Sound Regional Planning Commission.

4-344   TFN Profile. (Revised) (1985). Ottawa, Ontario: Tungavik Federation of
        Nunavut.

        Outline of the aims, organization, functions and membership of the
        Tungavik Federation of Nunavut.

4-345   TFN Recommends Changes to Gov't Policy. (1985, November). Nunavut, 4(6),
        2-3.

        List of the recommendations made by the Tungavik Federation of Nunavut
        for changes to federal government policy on landclaims, (including
        alternatives to extinguishment of title) in both content and implementation.

4-346   TFN Tables Marine Area Provisions. (1986, November). Nunavut, 5(11), 5.

        Statement by the Tungavik Federation of Nunavut of its intention to
        negotiate for inclusion of the offshore areas of Nunavut in any landclaim
        settlement.

4-347   TFN Takes Stand Against Sale. (1984, November). Nunavut, 3(9), 2.

        Concerns over possible sale of municipal lands before the land identification
        process has been completed in Nunavut.

4-348   TFN Update: Claims Update. (1988, March). Building Blocks, (8), 3-4.

        Summary of the progress of the Tungavik Federation of Nunavut claim, list
        of documents initialed to date, and schedule of negotiations.

4-349   TFN Votes Against $7.5 Million Loan. (1983, July). Nunavut Newsletter, 5-7.

        Decision by Tungavik Federation of Nunavut to refuse the guarantee of a
        bank loan to the Nunasi Development Corporation, in order to avoid using
        landclaims compensation money before a settlement is reached. Includes
        text of Board resolution.

4-350   TFN Waits to See Where the Foot Will Fall. (1987, May). Nunavut., 6(5), 2.

        Account of Tungavik Federation of Nunavut position on the new Federal
        Government policy on landclaims as it relates to Nunavut, the offshore,
        wildlife harvesting and other issues.

4-351   Tour Gives Clearer Picture of Land Claims. (1984, May). Nunavut Newsletter,
        3(3), 2-7.

        Account of tour of the Kitikmeot (Central Arctic) region by the negotiators
        for TFN (Tungavik Federation of Nunavut) to hold public meetings in
        Cambridge Bay, Pelly Bay, Gjoa Haven, Spence Bay, Coppermine and
        Holman Island, to explain the Nunavut landclaims proposals and process,
        including compensation, eligibility, extinguishment, land ownership and
        management, and the offshore.

4-352   Tungavik Federation of Nunavut (1984). Brief to the Commission of Inquiry on Equality in Employment. s.l.: Tungavik Federation of Nunavut.

Brief to the Commission outlining the circumstances and choices confronting Inuit living in Nunavut by reviewing the specific initiatives already underway to realize the goals and aspirations of Inuit, by discussing in detail the barriers and limitations of existing employment and training programs and policies affecting Inuit, and by identifying proposed alternatives.

4-353   Tungavik Federation of Nunavut. (1989, January). An Inuit Response. Northern Perspectives, 17(1), 15-18.

Reply to the "Irwin Report" (Lords of the Arctic, Wards of the State, by Colin Irwin) on the future of Inuit society and the prospects for Nunavut, affirming the agenda for division of the Northwest Territories, continuity of cultural tradition, and a hunter income support program.

4-354   Tungavik Federation of Nunavut. (1987). Land Claims, National Parks, Protected Areas and Renewable Resource Economy. In J. G. Nelson, R. Needham, & L. Norton (Editors), Arctic Heritage: Proceedings of a Symposium August 24-28, 1985 Banff, Alberta, Canada, (pp. 285-297). Ottawa, Ont.: Association of Canadian Universities for Northern Studies.

Outlines the aims of the Nunavut Land Claims Project and the scope of the Inuit claim and involvement in the management of natural resources.

4-355   Tungavik Federation of Nunavut (1984). Preparing For the Settlement: A Training Proposal Submitted by the Tungavik Federation of Nunavut to the Canada Employment and Immigration Commission. Ottawa, Ont.: Inuit Tapirisat of Canada.

The TFN proposes to conduct a ten-month (42 week) training program designed to equip ten Inuit with the knowledge and skills needed to qualify for positions as Community Liaison Workers with the TFN-positions which will exist until such time as a final agreement is reached.

4-356   Tungavik Federation of Nunavut. (1983, July). Nunavut Newsletter, 15.

List of members and staff of TFN (Tungavik Federation of Nunavut).

4-357   Tungavik Federation of Nunavut. (1984, August 14). Northern Decisions, 2(8), 53.

Announcement of agreement on provisions for land use planning in Nunavut, between the Tungavik Federation of Nunavut, and Indian and Northern Affairs Canada.

4-358   Tungavik Federation of Nunavut. (1985, January 31). Northern Decisions, 2(18), 125.

Announcement of agreement to establish the Nunavut Water Board.

4-359   Tungavik Federation of Nunavut. (1986, May 31). <u>Northern Decisions</u>, 4(4), 31.

Announcement of the initialing of an Agreement-in-Principle on wildlife provisions for Nunavut (guarantee of harvesting rights and creation of a Wildlife Management Board), by the federal government and the Tungavik Federation of Nunavut.

4-360   Tungavik Federation of Nunavut. (1986, October 15). <u>Northern Decisions</u>, 4(12), 88.

Announcement of the tabling of a position paper "Marine Area Provisions" of an Agreement-in-Principle, by the Tungavik Federation of Nunavut, proposing application of land and resource positions already negotiated to marine areas, and the creation of a Nunavut marine council.

4-361   Tungavik Federation of Nunavut. (1987, March 31). <u>Northern Decisions</u>, 4(22), 168.

Notice of Inuit ratification, through the Tungavik Federation of Nunavut (TFN), of the May 1980 landclaims and overlap boundary agreement.

4-362   Tungavik Federation of Nunavut. (1987, May 31). <u>Northern Decisions</u>, 5(4), 35.

Announcement of start of negotiations between the Tungavik Federation of Nunavut (TFN) and the federal government of Canada, on 25 June, 1987, at Pangnirtung, Northwest Territories, concerning the offshore.

4-363   Tungavik Federation of Nunavut. (1988, January 15). <u>Northern Decisions</u>, 5(17), 152.

Announcement of approval by the Federal Cabinet of a mandate for negotiations of the Tungavik Federation of Nunavut comprehensive land claim, including Inuit rights in the offshore and participation in decision making on environmental matters.

4-364   Tungavik Federation of Nunavut. (1988, April 15). <u>Northern Decisions</u>, 6(1), 5.

Announcement of the signing of a memorandum of understanding between the Tungavik Federation of Nunavut (TFN) and the Government of the Northwest Territories, to cooperate in establishing a Northern Energy Accord.

4-365   Tungavik Federation of Nunavut. (1988, May 15). <u>Northern Decisions</u>, 6(3), 24.

Announcement of the first negotiating session (May 3-4, 1988) between the Tungavik Federation of Nunavut (TFN) and the Makivik Corporation on a boundary and joint management overlap agreement for the Hudson Bay/Hudson Strait offshore area.

4-366   Tungavik Federation of Nunavut. (1988, June 15). <u>Northern Decisions</u>, 6(5), 39.

> Initialing on June 6, 1988 of a paper concerning title to Inuit lands, by the Tungavik Federation of Nunavut and the federal government, describing forms of title and rights to carving stone and other materials.

4-367   Tungavik Federation of Nunavut. (1988, June 30). <u>Northern Decisions</u>, 6(6), 49.

> Initialing on June 19, 1988 of the Agreement-in-Principle between the Tungavik Federation of Nunavut (TFN) and the federal government on wildlife compensation.

4-368   Tungavik Federation of Nunavut. (1988, July 15). <u>Northern Decisions</u>, 6(7), 56.

> Initialing on July 11, 1988 by the Tungavik Federation of Nunavut (TFN) and the federal government of an Agreement-in-Principle on the ratification provisions of an overall Agreement-in-Principle.

4-369   Tungavik Federation of Nunavut. (1988, September 15). <u>Northern Decisions</u>, 6(10), 79-80.

> Initialing on August 29, 1988, of an Agreement-in-Principle on implementation provisions for an overall Agreement-in-Principle between negotiators for the Tungavik Federation of Nunavut (TFN) and the federal government.

4-370   Tungavik Federation of Nunavut. (1988, October 31). <u>Northern Decisions </u>, 6(13), 102.

> Talks to begin in November 1988 between the Tungavik Federation of Nunavut (TFN) and the federal Government to determine the total amount of Inuit land under the Nunavut landclaim settlement.

4-371   Tungavik Federation of Nunavut. (1988, December 15). <u>Northern Decisions</u>, 6(16), 126.

> Signing on December 13, 1988, by the Tungavik Federation of Nunavut (TFN) and the federal government, of an Agreement-in-Principle on development impact and screening provisions of an overall agreement, including establishment of the Nunavut Impact Review Board.

4-372   Tungavik Federation of Nunavut. (1989, February 15). <u>Northern Decisions</u>, 6(19), 146.

> Signing, on February 13, 1989, of an Agreement-in-Principle on a land quantum for the Sanikiluaq region, by the Tungavik Federation of Nunavut (TFN) and the federal government.

4-373   Tungavik Federation of Nunavut. (1989, February 28). Northern Decisions, 6(20), 153.

Initialing, on February 17, 1989, of the landclaim document "Social Provisions of an Agreement-in-Principle" by the Tungavik Federation of Nunavut (TFN) and the federal government. Announcement of negotiations on economic provisions and wildlife compensation as they pertain to the offshore, to be held March 8-15, 1989.

4-374   Tungavik Federation of Nunavut. (1989, April 30). Northern Decisions, 7(2), 12.

Tabling on April 11, 1989, by the Tungavik Federation of Nunavut (TFN) of an economic package consisting of resource revenue sharing, subsurface quantum, and capital transfer (cash compensation).

4-375   Tungavik Federation of Nunavut. (1989, December 15). Northern Decisions, 7(16), 122.

Tentative Land Claim Agreement-in-Principle, for the settlement of the Inuit landclaim in the eastern Arctic signed by the Tungavik Federation of Nunavut (TFN) and the federal government.

4-376   Tungavik Federation of Nunavut Response to Concerns Raised in the Assembly Respecting the Inuit Impact and Benefit Agreements Provisions of an Agreement in Principle. (1988). Yellowknife, N.W.T.: Government of the Northwest Territories.

Tabled document no. 35-86(1) tabled on March 4, 1986. This open letter to the people of the Northwest Territories, from the Tungavik Federation of Nunavut, attempts to clarify the Federation's position on landclaims negotiations and on the Inuit Impact and Benefits Agreement.

4-377   Tungavik Federation of Nunavut (TFN) Claim: Claims Update. (1987, May). Building Blocks, (6), 3.

Report of the initialing of a sub-agreement on "Eligibility and Enrollment" to establish a beneficiary list and a Nunavut Appeal Board. Also discusses the development of a discussion paper to form the basis of a sub-agreement on the Nunavut Impact Review Board, and the tabling of a discussion paper on the Land Identification Process.

4-378   Tungavik Federation of Nunavut (TFN) Comprehensive Claim: Northwest Territories. (1989). Information Sheet (Canada. Indian and Northern Affairs Canada), 1989:8. Ottawa, Ont.: Indian and Northern Affairs Canada.

Brief background and chronology of the landclaim by the Tungavik Federation of Nunavut representing Inuit residents of the Northwest Territories.

4-379   Tungavik Federation of Nunavut (TFN) Comprehensive Claim: Northwest
        Territories. (1990). Information Sheet (Canada. Indian and Northern
        Affairs Canada), 1990:8. Ottawa, Ont.: Indian and Northern Affairs Canada.

        Brief background and chronology of the land claim by the Tungavik
        Federation of Nunavut representing Inuit residents of the Northwest
        Territories.

4-380   Tunraluk, A. (1987). Managerial Training in Nunasi Corporation. In W. P.
        Adams (Editor), Education, Research, Information Systems and the North,
        (pp. 101-102). Ottawa, Ont.: Association of Canadian Universities for
        Northern Studies.

        This article provides background information about the Nunasi
        Corporation, the business arm of the Inuit of Nunavut, and describes the
        "Nunasi Careers Program" that it proposed to Canada Employment and
        Immigration to meet their target number of Inuit managers.

4-381   Urgency of Preparing For Land Claims Has Never Been So Great. (1984,
        January). Nunasi Report, 1(1), 8.

        Editorial explaining the need for business experience for Inuit, in
        preparation for managing and investing moneys resulting from landclaims
        settlements for Nunavut.

4-382   Usher, P. J. (1986). Affidavit: Re Tungavik Federation of Nunavut re Prince
        Albert Tribal Council. Ottawa, Ont.: Nelligan-Power Law Offices.

        Draft text of a consultant's opinion on the evidence of Indian (Denesutine)
        and Inuit use of areas in the southern Keewatin, Northwest Territories,
        which was claimed by Inuit as part of Nunavut and disputed by the Indian
        bands of northern Manitoba and Saskatchewan.

4-383   Usher, P. J., & Bankes, N. D. (1986). Property, the Basis of Inuit Hunting
        Rights: A New Approach. Ottawa, Ont.: Inuit Committee on National
        Issues.

        Proposes a new approach to aboriginal hunting, fishing and trapping rights,
        exposing the inadequacies of traditional political and legal perspectives on
        renewable resource rights. Suggests that by using a concept familiar in
        Anglo-Canadian property law, that of profit-a-prendre, these inadequacies
        can be overcome, providing more security to aboriginal people and more
        clarity in judicial decision-making.

4-384   Viewpoint North: Constitutional Development in the N.W.T.: a Discussion.
        (1985, March). Information North, (1), 2-6.

        In January 1985, the Constitutional Alliance of the Northwest Territories
        reached a tentative agreement on a boundary for division of the Territories
        into two separate northern territories. (The Alliance comprises the Western
        Constitutional Forum (WCF) and the Nunavut Constitutional Forum (NCF).

4-385   Views Differ on the Impact of N.W.T. Division. (1983, January). <u>Nunavut Newsletter</u>, 8.

Discussion of whether the Federal Government agreement of November, 1982 on division of the Northwest Territories would affect the mandate of the Chief Negotiator on the Nunavut landclaim.

4-386   Vontobel, R. (1991, August). Western Boundary Question is Resolved. <u>Nunavut</u>, 10(34).

Announcement of the signing of an agreement between the Tungavik Federation on Nunavut and the Minister of Indian Affairs and Northern Development on the western boundary of Nunavut.

4-387   Water Provisions in Nunavut and Inuit Water Rights. (1986, August). <u>Building Blocks</u>, (4), 2.

Summary of the sub-agreements on water provisions establishing the Nunavut Water Board.

4-388   <u>Water Provisions of an Agreement-in-Principle</u>. (1985). Ottawa, Ont.: Tungavik Federation of Nunavut.

Draft provisions of Part 8, Water Use and Disposition, of the Nunavut Agreement, including creation of Nunavut Water Board.

4-389   Water Rights are Protected in New Agreement. (1986, January). <u>Nunavut</u>, 5(1), 2.

Announcement of agreement between the Federal Government of Canada and Tungavik Federation of Nunavut, on "Provisions for Inuit Water Rights".

4-390   Weihs, F. (1986). <u>Economic Resources Package Discussion Paper: Overview of the Economic Resources Package of the Nunavut Claim</u>. Ottawa, Ont.: Fred Weihs.

This paper examines and evaluates the general approach taken to economic aspects of the Nunavut claim, including relevancy, completeness, and complementarity to areas already negotiated.

4-391   Weihs, F. (1986, February). Hunters Face Escalating Costs. <u>Nunavut</u>, 5(2), 2.

Discussion of ways in which a Nunavut landclaim settlement could give greater economic security to hunters in the face of rising costs.

4-392   Weller, G. R. (1988). Self-Government For Canada's Inuit: The Nunavut Proposal. <u>American Review of Canadian Studies</u>, 18(3), 341-358.

A review of the development of the concept of Nunavut, with a summary of arguments for and against its creation.

4-393   What is Nunavut Trust, and Their Responsibilities? (1992, November). <u>Nunavut</u>,
        11(6), 24.

        Explanation of the structure, role and powers of the Nunavut Trust which
        holds moneys for development of the new territory.

4-394   Whittington, M. S., & MacPherson, S. (1983). <u>Division of the N.W.T.:</u>
        <u>Administration Structures for Nunavut. Report of the Sub-Committee on</u>
        <u>Division, Legislative Assembly of the N.W.T.: Executive Summary.</u>
        Yellowknife, N.W.T: The Committee.

        A report on the research of the design of basic administrative structures for
        the political division of the N.W.T., providing a tentative blueprint for the
        Nunavut bureaucracy in the form of a complete set of organizational charts
        for the government department that will be required.

4-395   Who is Representing You on TFN'S Board? (1986, January). <u>Nunavut</u>, 5(1), 10.

        Chart of membership of the Board of the Tungavik Federation of Nunavut.

4-396   Who Owns What? TFN Needs Answers Now to Crucial Questions. (1987,
        September). <u>Nunavut</u>, 6(7), 2.

        Summaries of progress in negotiations on Inuit ownership of land in
        Nunavut: on natural resource management: on bodies with guaranteed Inuit
        representation (Nunavut Wildlife Management Board, Nunavut Land Use
        Planning Commission, Nunavut Impact Review Board, Nunavut Water
        Board, and Inuit Impact and Benefit Agreements (IIBA's): on the Northern
        Inland Waters Act, and on the Lancaster Sound Regional Planning
        Commission.

4-397   Who Will Be a Member of NIRB? (1989, December). <u>Nunavut</u>, 8(1), 2-10.

        Summary of the Development Impact Provisions of an Agreement-in-
        Principle: Screening and Review of Project Proposals and Applications
        (NIRB or Nunavut Impact Review Board Agreement), concerning land use,
        economic development and the environmental impact assessment process.

4-398   Who will Benefit from Land Claims? (1986, May). <u>Nunavut</u>, 5(5), 9.

        Explanation of the proposed criteria and procedures for eligibility and
        enrollment in Nunavut.

4-399   Why are Negotiations Taking so Long? (1983, August). <u>Nunavut Newsletter</u>,
        12-14.

        Summary of progress to date on landclaims negotiations for Nunavut.

4-400   Wildlife Agreement Re-Initialed After Five Years Dormant: TFN Claim. (1986, June). Building Blocks, (2), 1.

Discussion of the re-initialing of the Tungavik Federation of Nunavut Wildlife Agreement, which covers creation of a Nunavut Wildlife Management Board, Inuit harvesting rights, and Inuit economic opportunities.

4-401   Wonders, W. C. (1988). Overlapping Native Land Claims in the Northwest Territories. American Review of Canadian Studies, 18(3), 359-368.

Review and discussion of the areas in the Northwest Territories claimed by both Inuit and Dene/Metis groups as part of Denendeh and Nunavut respectively.

SECTION 5: COMPARATIVE STUDIES - CANADIAN

5-1   Aboriginal Land Claims in Canada. (1989). Information Sheet. (Canada. Indian and Northern Affairs Canada), 1989:1. Ottawa, Ont.: Indian and Northern Affairs Canada.

Outline of the procedure and policy for considering comprehensive and specific landclaims in Canada by Indian, Dene, Metis and Inuit groups.

5-2   Aboriginal Peoples and Resource Development: Conflict or Co-operation. (1991). Alternatives, 18(2), 1-49.

Articles dealing with aboriginal landclaims, resource management, and the James Bay project in northern Canada.

5-3   Aboriginal Self-Government. (1989). Information Sheet. (Canada. Indian and Northern Affairs Canada), 1989:3. Ottawa, Ont.: Indian and Northern Affairs Canada.

Definition and brief history of the concept of self-government for Indian, Inuit and Metis peoples in Canada, with summary of relevant legislation.

5-4   Aboriginal Self-Government. (1992). Current Issue Review. Ottawa, Ont.: Library of Parliament. Research Branch.

Provides a definition of the issue of aboriginal (Indian) self-government in Canada, with background and history leading to implementation of the Indian Act, Sechelt Act and agreements on landclaims including discussions on the national constitution. Continues Indian self-government.

5-5   Agreement in Principle Between the Dene Nation and Her Majesty the Queen in Right of Canada, Presented to the Federal Government on October 25, 1976. (1976). s.l.: s.n.

Discusses Dene Nation struggle for aboriginal rights in the Mackenzie Valley, N.W.T. and sets forth an agreement-in-principle which specifies the

principles which the Dene consider to be an essential basis for further
negotiations between Dene and Government of Canada.

5-6   Arctic Institute of North America. Sustainable Development Research Group
        (1989). Coping With the Cash: a Financial Review of Four Northern Land
        Claims Settlements With a View to Maximizing Economic Opportunities
        From the Next Generation of Claim Settlements in the Northwest
        Territories. Calgary, Alta.: Arctic Institute of North America.

        Reviews the economic impact of the Alaskan Settlement, the Inuvialuit
        Settlement, the James Bay Cree and the Northern Quebec Inuit Settlements.
        The authors then provide some estimates of the potential impacts of the
        N.W.T. settlements based upon different ways the beneficiaries might
        choose to use and distribute their resources.

5-7   Asch, M. (1983). Aboriginal Rights and the Calder Case in Anthropological
        Perspective. Recherches Amerindiennes au Quebec, 13(3), 169-178.

        An analysis of how, and in accordance with what criteria, the courts of the
        British Empire, particularly those of Australia and Canada, have approached
        the analysis and definition of aboriginal rights.

5-8   Asch, M., & Smith, S. (1992). Consociation Revisited: Nunavut, Denendeh and
        Canadian Constitutional Consciousness. Etudes Inuit Studies, 16(1-2), 97-
        114.

        Addresses the question of how the ethnonational rights of the Dene, Metis,
        Inuit, Inuvialiut and non-aboriginal populations will be addressed in the
        context of the division of the N.W.T into two new territories. A method for
        differentiating the ideological orientations of the Nunavut and Denendeh
        proposals in the area of the protection of ethnonational rights is reviewed.
        The authors then discuss how each of these proposals would address
        specific powers, how the proposals have been received and some likely
        possibilities for future developments.

5-9   Bankes, N. (1983). Resource-Leasing Options and the Settlement of Aboriginal
        Claims. Ottawa, Ont.: Canadian Arctic Resources Committee.

        An examination of a variety of leasing arrangements between resource
        development companies and aboriginal groups to demonstrate the options
        available to native peoples attempting to gain control over resource
        development on their lands. Among others, examines in detail the Alaska
        Native Claims Settlement Act and the James Bay and Northern Quebec
        Agreement.

5-10   Berger, T. R. (1977). Northern Frontier, Northern Homeland: the Report of the
        Mackenzie Valley Pipeline Inquiry. Toronto, Ont.: James Lorimer.

        Originally published in 1977 as Report of Mackenzie Valley Pipeline Inquiry
        incorporating new introduction by Berger. A two volume report dealing
        with the broad social, economic, and environmental impacts that a gas
        pipeline and an energy corridor would have in the Mackenzie Valley and the
        western arctic.

5-11   Berger, T. R. (1985). <u>Village Journey: The Report of the Alaska Native Review Commission</u>. New York: Hill and Wang.

Report of Berger's review of the Alaska Native Claims Settlement Act of 1971. Besides analyzing ANCSA, Berger also addresses other questions such as land, subsistence, and the future of the villages which were raised by Alaskan natives during his travels around Alaska.

5-12   Bilson, B. (1976). Aboriginal Hunting Rights: Some Issues Raised by the Case of R. v. Frank. <u>Saskatchewan Law Review</u>, 41(1), 101-124.

Discussion concerning the rights of Indians to hunt at anytime on reserve lands, in the context of native rights to traditional homelands.

5-13   Braden, G. (1976). <u>The Emergence of Native Interest Groups and Their Impact on the Political and Economic Development of the Northwest Territories, 1969 to 1975</u>. Masters Thesis. Dalhousie University, Dept. of Political Science, Dalhousie, N.B.

Focuses on the emergence, behavior and impact of four N.W.T. native interest groups: Indian Brotherhood of the N.W.T.; Metis Association of the N.W.T.; Inuit Tapirisat of Canada; and Committee For Original Peoples' Entitlement.

5-14   Canada. Dept. of Indian Affairs and Northern Development (1988). <u>Comprehensive Land Claim Agreement in Principle Between Canada and the Dene Nation and the Metis Association of the Northwest Territories</u>. Ottawa, Ont.: Dept. of Indian Affairs and Northern Development.

Text of the agreement-in-principle. Includes sections on financial, renewable resources, land and resources, administration of lands and resources, relationship with other claimants.

5-15   Canada. Dept. of Indian Affairs and Northern Development (1989). <u>Comprehensive Land Claim Agreement in Principle Between the Government of Canada, the Council for Yukon Indians and Government of the Yukon</u>. Ottawa, Ont.: Dept. of Indian Affairs and Northern Development.

Lists the agreement and sub-agreements in relation to land, renewable resources, financial obligations, Yukon Indian self-government, and others.

5-16   Canada. Dept. of Indian Affairs and Northern Development (1978). <u>Dene and Metis Claims in the Mackenzie Valley: Proposals for Discussion</u>. Yellowknife, N.W.T.: Canada. Department of Indian Affairs and Northern Development.

Proposals put forward to the Metis Association of the Northwest Territories and to the Indian Brotherhood of the Northwest Territories by Keith Penner, M.P.

5-17   Canada. Dept. of Indian Affairs and Northern Development (1981). Federal
        Native Claims Policy: Summary of Policy Statement of August 8, 1973.
        Ottawa, Ont.: Canada Department of Indian Affairs and Northern
        Development.

        Contains information sheets about Federal Native Claims Policy in Canada.
        Topics include: summary of 1973 policy statement, description of claims
        process, role and responsibilities of Office of Native Claims, history of
        mechanisms for dealing with native claims, and funding for native claims.
        Also provides chronological summaries of claims in Labrador, Nova Scotia,
        Quebec, B.C., Mackenzie Valley, and Yukon as well as claims of the
        Committee for Original Peoples' Entitlement.

5-18   Canada. Dept. of Indian Affairs and Northern Development (1981). In All
        Fairness: a Native Claims Policy: Comprehensive Claims = En toute
        Justice: une Politique des Revendications des Autochtones: Revendications
        Globales. Ottawa, Ont.: Indian and Northern Affairs Canada.

        For some years past, the Government of Canada has been engaged in
        attempting to resolve what have come to be known as Comprehensive
        Native Land Claims, through a negotiation process. There has been
        moderate success but much more remains to be done. The purpose of this
        book is to set out for the consideration of all Canadians what the
        government proposes as the way forward.

5-19   Canada. Dept. of Indian Affairs and Northern Development (1984). Indian Self-
        Government in Canada: Report of the Special Committee. s.l.: Dept. of
        Indian Affairs and Northern Development.

        Briefly describes the report of the House of Commons Special Committee
        on Indian Self-Government in Canada. Includes membership, mandate,
        process, and recommendations. (Known as the "Penner Committee").

5-20   Canada. Dept. of Indian Affairs and Northern Development (1983). Minister's
        letter: a Letter to Indian People on Current Issues From the Minister of
        Indian Affairs and Northern Development = Lettre du Ministre: Lettre du
        Ministre des Affaires Indiennes et du Nord Canadien Aux Indiens, Sur des
        Question D'Actualite. Ottawa, Ont.: Department of Indian Affairs and
        Northern Development.

        Discusses aboriginal rights and the Canadian Constitution. Includes a copy
        of the 1983 Constitutional Accord on Aboriginal Rights.

5-21   Canada. Dept. of Indian Affairs and Northern Development (1982). Outstanding
        Business: a Native Claims Policy: Specific Claims. Ottawa, Ont.:
        Department of Indian Affairs and Northern Development.

        Outlines Canadian government policy on native claims, and enunciates
        guidelines regarding the basis for specific claims, operation of the claims
        process and assessment of claims and compensation.

5-22   Canada. Dept. of Indian Affairs and Northern Development (1983). <u>Specific</u>
        <u>Claims in Canada: Status Report</u>. Ottawa, Ontario: Department of Indian
        Affairs and Northern Development.

        Lists native claims in Canada by province, indicating band, substance of
        claim, status of claim and last action taken.

5-23   Canada. Dept. of Indian Affairs and Northern Development. Office of Native
        Claims (1980). <u>Native Claims in Canada: a Summary, on an Element-By-</u>
        <u>Element Basis, of Comprehensive Native Claim Proposals That Have Been</u>
        <u>Presented to the Federal Government and of Native Claim Settlements</u>.
        s.l.: s.n.

        Contains summaries of the following native claims and claims settlements in
        Canada: Gitksan-Carrier Band, Kitwancool Band, Labrador-Inuit
        Association, Naskapi-Montagnais Innu Association, Conseil Attikamek-
        Montagnais du Quebec, Nishga Tribal Council, Inuit Tapirisat of Canada,
        Council for Yukon Indians, James Bay and Northern Quebec Agreement
        (Grand Council of Crees of Quebec, Northern Quebec Inuit Association),
        Northeastern Quebec Agreement (Naskapis of Schefferville Band), Metis
        Association of the Northwest Territories, Dene Nation, and Committee for
        Original Peoples' Entitlement. Arranged in columnar format with element
        by element analysis.

5-24   Canada. Dept. of Indian Affairs and Northern Development (1984). <u>The</u>
        <u>Western Arctic Claim: a Guide to the Inuvialuit Final Agreement</u> = la
        <u>Revendication de l'Arctique de l'Quest: Guide Explicatif de l'Entente Finale</u>
        <u>des Inuvialuit</u>. Ottawa, Ont.: Department of Indian Affairs and Northern
        Development.

        A general guide to the final agreement on settlement of the Western Arctic
        Claim.

5-25   Canada. Dept. of Indian Affairs and Northern Development (1984). <u>The Western</u>
        <u>Arctic Claim: the Inuvialuit Final Agreement</u>. Ottawa, Ont.: Department of
        Indian Affairs and Northern Development.

        Final settlement between COPE (the Committee for Original Peoples'
        Entitlement), and the Government of Canada. Land settlement includes the
        north slope of Yukon Territory.

5-26   Canada. Dept. of Indian Affairs and Northern Development (1982). <u>Yukon</u>
        <u>Indian Claim Agreement in Principle: General Summary</u>. Whitehorse, Yukon:
        Department of Indian Affairs and Northern Development.

        Briefly summarizes the following aspects of the Yukon Indian Claim
        Agreement-in-Principle: financial compensation, lands, government
        program, land use planning and environmental assessment, hunting, fishing
        and trapping rights, and finality.

5-27   Canada. Indian and Northern Affairs Canada <u>The James Bay and Northern</u>
        <u>Quebec Agreement, the Northeastern Quebec Agreement, Annual Report</u>.
        (1986-) Ottawa, Ont.: Indian and Northern Affairs Canada.

        Annual report on progress made in implementation of the James Bay and
        Northern Quebec Native Claims Settlement Act, the James Bay and
        Northern Quebec Agreement (JBNQA) and the Northeastern Quebec
        Agreement (NEQA) and the changes made in Cree, Inuit and Naskapi
        communities as a result.

5-28   Canada. Indian Claims Commission (1992). <u>Indian Claims Commission</u>. Ottawa,
        Ont.: The Commission.

        Outline of the purposes and work of the Indian Claims Commission,
        including terms of reference, membership and details of application for a
        consideration or review of a claim or for mediation.

5-29   Canada. Parliament . House of Commons. (1984). <u>Bill C-49. An Act to</u>
        <u>Approve, Give Effect to and Declare Valid the Agreement Between the</u>
        <u>Committee for Original Peoples' Entitlement, Representing the Inuvialuit of</u>
        <u>the Inuvialuit Settlement Region, and the Government of Canada and to</u>
        <u>Amend the National Parks Act in Consequence Thereof.</u> Ottawa, Ont.:
        Queen's Printer.

        Text of Bill C-49 or Western Arctic (Inuvialuit) Claims Settlement Act.
        Relates to agreement between Committee for Original Peoples' Entitlement
        and Government of Canada regarding land in N.W.T. and Yukon claimed by
        Inuvialuit.

5-30   Canada. Parliament. House of Commons. Special Committee on Indian Self-
        Government (1983). <u>Minutes of Proceedings of the Special Committee on</u>
        <u>Indian Self-Government Respecting the Status, Development and</u>
        <u>Responsibilities of Band Governments ... </u>. Ottawa, Ont.: Supply and
        Services Canada.

        Second report to the House respecting the status, development and
        responsibilities of band governments on Indian reserves, as well as the
        financial relationships between the Government of Canada and Indian bands.
        (Known as the "Penner Committee".)

5-31   Canada. Parliament. Senate. Task Force on the Meech Lake Constitutional
        Accord and on the Yukon and the Northwest Territories (1988). <u>Task Force</u>
        <u>on the Meech Lake Constitutional Accord and on the Yukon and the</u>
        <u>Northwest Territories: a Report of the Task Force to the Committee of the</u>
        <u>Whole</u>. Ottawa, Ont.: Queen's Printer.

        Tabled document no. 80-88(1) tabled on March 1, 1988. This report
        summarizes the views expressed by residents of the Yukon and Northwest
        Territories on the proposed status of the region under the new constitutional
        settlement in Canada.

5-32   Canadian Arctic Resources Committee. (1985, November). CARC's Brief to the
        Task Force on Native Claims Policy. Northern Perspectives, 13(5), 1-12.

        Presents the Canadian Arctic Resources Committee's submission to the
        Department of Indian Affairs and Northern Development concerning the
        settlement of landclaims on the federal territories north of the 60th parallel.

5-33   Cassidy, F. (1991). Reaching Just Settlements: Land Claims in British Columbia:
        Proceedings of a Conference Held February 21-22, 1990. Lantzville, B.C.,
        Halifax, Nova Scotia : Oolichan Books and The Institute for Research on
        Public Policy.

        A collection of papers representing the views of native, business, labor,
        municipal, and academic leaders in British Columbia on the need for and
        possible shape of just landclaims settlements in that province.

5-34   Chretien, J. (1969). Statement by the Honourable Jean Chretien, Minister of
        Indian Affairs and Northern Development, based on a speech delivered in
        Regina, October 2, 1969 = Declaration De L'Honorable Jean Chretien,
        Ministre des Affaires Indiennes et du Nord Canadien, en Mage d'un
        Discours qu'il a Prononce a Regina, lez octobre 1969. Ottawa, Ont.: Dept.
        of Indian Affairs and Northern Development .

        Transcript of speech by Jean Chretien in which he explains the federal
        government's Indian Policy Statement and enunciates principal elements of
        Indian Policy proposals. Based on "White Paper".

5-35   Committee for Original Peoples' Entitlement (1977). Inuvialuit Nunangat:
        Background Papers. Inuvik, N.W.T.: The Committee.

        Series of working papers providing background information for Inuvialuit
        Nunangat (settlement of Inuvialuit landclaims in the western Arctic).

5-36   Committee for Original Peoples' Entitlement (1977). "Inuvialuit Nunungat": the
        Proposal for an Agreement in Principle to Achieve the Settlement of
        Inuvialuit Land Rights in the Western Arctic Region of the Northwest and
        Yukon Territories Between the Government of Canada and the Committee
        for Original Peoples' Entitlement. s.l.: Committee for Original Peoples'
        Entitlement.

        COPE proposal for a settlement of landclaims in the western Canadian
        Arctic encompassing the Mackenzie Delta, Banks Island, and parts of the
        High Arctic.

5-37   Committee for Original Peoples' Entitlement (1978). Inuvialuit Land Rights
        Settlement Agreement in Principle = Reglement de la Revendication
        Fonciere des Inuvialuit Entente de Principe = Inuvialuit Nunangata San-
        Naiyaota Sivol-Lek Ilogaagun. Ottawa, Ont.: s.n.

        Text of the Agreement-in-Principle between the Committee for Original
        Peoples' Entitlement (COPE) and the Government of Canada represented
        by the Minister of Indian Affairs and Northern Development, on land rights
        in the Inuvialuit (Western Arctic/ Mackenzie Delta) region of the Northwest

Territories, including land selection, wildlife status, financial compensation, economic measures, and form of government.

5-38   Comprehensive Land Claims Policy = la Politique des Revendications Territoriales Globales. (1987). Ottawa, Ont.: Canada. Indian and Northern Affairs Canada.

Booklet which sets out the elements of the revised federal comprehensive landclaims policy as presented in the House of Commons on December 18, 1986. Organized in six main sections: objectives; scope of negotiations; self-government; involvement of provincial and territorial governments; protection of aboriginal and non-aboriginal interests; and procedures. (Known as the Blue Book.)

5-39   Comprehensive Land Claim Umbrella Final Agreement Between the Government of Canada, the Council for Yukon Indians and the Government of the Yukon. (1990). Ottawa, Ont.: s.n.

Text of an agreement recommended for ratification by the negotiators for the Council for Yukon Indians, Government of Canada and Government of the Yukon to settle landclaims by Yukon First Nations.

5-40   COPE Final Agreement is Now Legislation. (1984, July). Nunavut Newsletter, 3(5), 6.

Summary, with map, of the Inuvialuit Final Agreement settled by the Committee For Original People's Entitlement (COPE) in the western Arctic.

5-41   COPE - Government Working Group Joint Position Paper on Wildlife. (1977). Ottawa, Ont.: s.n.

Joint position paper which sets out areas relating to the arctic wildlife component of the landclaim of the Committee For Original Peoples' Entitlement where agreement has been reached between COPE's representatives and Canadian government officials.

5-42   The COPE/Government Working Group Joint Position Paper on the Inuvialuit Land Rights Claim = COPELU/Govermatlu Sanigaani Kavaktingit Tamkmik Sivok - Kiotaat Makpigak Inuvialuit Nunangat Okasogigiga - Mitjong. (1978). s.l.: s.n.

Joint position paper regarding COPE'S landclaims in the western Canadian Arctic.

5-43   Council for Yukon Indians Comprehensive Land Claim. (1989). Information Sheet. (Canada. Indian and Northern Affairs Canada), 1989:18. Ottawa, Ont.: Indian and Northern Affairs Canada.

Summary of the comprehensive claims process in the Yukon and brief history of the Agrement-in-Principle, the Yukon Native Brotherhood (YNB), Yukon Association for Non-Status Indians (YANSI) and the Council for Yukon Indians (CYI).

5-44   Crowe, K. J. (1979). A Summary of Northern Native Claims in Canada: the Process and Progress of Negotiations. Etudes Inuit, 3(1), 31-39.

A settlement of Alaska native claims in 1971 gave impetus to a similar movement in Canada. The official process is described for comprehensive claims, involving first a stage of classification then a stage of actual negotiation. Comprehensive claims that have been filed so far are examined, including those of the Council for Yukon Indians, Inuit Tapirisat of Canada and the Committee for Original Peoples' Entitlement.

5-45   Dacks, G. (1985). Consensus Government in the Northwest Territories. Annual Meeting of the Canadian Political Science Association, Montreal, Que., 1985, May 31. s.l.: s.n.

Paper presented to the annual meeting of the Canadian Political Science Association which reviews consensus politics in two northern contexts in the N.W.T: that of traditional Dene practice and that of the Legislative Assembly of the N.W.T.

5-46   Dacks, G. (1984). Liberal-Democratic Society and Government in Canada. Yellowknife, N.W.T.: Western Constitutional Forum.

Argues that a government only works well if it reflects the values and assumptions of the society which it rules and questions whether the liberal-democratic government found in the provinces is the best model on which to base a new government system for the western Northwest Territories.

5-47   Dacks, G. (1986). Politics on the Last Frontier: Consociationalism in the Northwest Territories. Canadian Journal of Political Science, 19(2), 345-361.

Note which focuses on the western portion of the Northwest Territories. Argues that the social bias for consensus politics is absent and that present practice in the Legislative Assembly of the N.W.T. owes more to non-partisanship than to consensus. Argues that, whatever the format of the Assembly, consociationalism, including significant devolution of power to local governments, represents the most promising direction to explore because it reflects NWT's social structure and addresses the fundamental concerns of the cultural communities.

5-48   Dacks, G. (1990). Political and Constitutional Development in the Yukon and the Northwest Territories: the Influence of Devolution. Northern Review, 5, 102-130.

Examines how devolution of jurisdiction from government of Canada to territorial governments is affecting linked processes of constitutional and political development in northern Canada.

5-49   Dene and Metis Comprehensive Land Claim. (1989). Information Sheet. (Canada. Indian and Northern Affairs Canada), 1989:22. Ottawa, Ont.: Indian and Northern Affairs Canada.

Outline of the comprehensive landclaim filed by the Dene and Metis peoples of the western part of the Northwest Territories (Mackenzie Valley) with the Federal Government of Canada.

5-50   Dene Declaration: Statement of Rights. (1975). s.l.: s.n.

Statement by the Dene (Indians) of the Northwest Territories on their right to self-determination and recognition as a nation, rather than as a group within the "Fourth World".

5-51   Dene Nation Annual Report. Yellowknife, N.W.T.: Dene Nation Communications Dept.

Details of the organization, finances, and activities of the Dene Nation (Indian residents of Denendeh, the western Northwest Territories), including chiefs of bands, landclaims, chronology, brief histories, and agendas and resolutions of the annual National Assembly.

5-52   Devine, M. (1993, March). The New Western Territory: Balkanization or Federation? Northern Perspectives, 21(1), 10-14.

The territorial government established the Commission for Constitutional Development in the summer of 1991 to "develop a comprehensive constitutional proposal for those regions of the Northwest Territories remaining after the creation of Nunavut for consideration by way of plebiscite". The Commission released its phase one report, " Working Toward a Common Future" in April 1992. In this article, the author outlines the commission's report and speculates as to its likely impact.

5-53   Diabo, R. (1987). Independent Analysis of the 1986 Comprehensive Land Claims Policy: Draft. Ottawa, Ont.: Institute of Canadian Studies, Carleton University.

Review of the "blue book" on government policy on landclaims , released in 1986, with discussion of implications for Indians and Inuit and of the procedures proposed for implementation.

5-54   DIAND Says "Offshore" Mandate Premature. (1986, January). Nunavut, 5(1), 5.

Comment on the question of whether offshore rights should be included in a landclaims settlement in Nunavut.

5-55   Elias, P. D. (1989, January). Aboriginal Rights and Litigation: History and Future of Court Decisions in Canada. Polar Record, 25(152), 1-8.

Recent decisions of the Supreme Court of Canada, the Constitution Act 1982, and the establishment of the Office of Native Claims, would seem to have assured the rapid settlement of outstanding issues regarding aboriginal rights and native title to lands. More recently, the seeming abandonment by government of political and negotiated resolution of these issues has left litigation as the remaining recourse for native groups to protect their interests. The courts, however, have become increasingly demanding in terms of what must be proven in order to make a successful case at law. This paper predicted that the costs and technical difficulties of providing such proofs will limit the number of rights cases before the courts, and the chances of success for those that are mounted.

5-56   The Evolution of Public Governments in the North and the Implications For Aboriginal Peoples. (1993). Ottawa, Ont.: Indian and Northern Affairs Canada.

This paper is intended to provide a historical perspective of the evolution of public government in the Yukon and Northwest Territories, and describes the relationships between Aboriginal organizations and the federal and territorial governments as these have developed over the last century in Canada, including Nunavut and other regional and local government models.

5-57   The Federal Comprehensive Claims Policy. (1987, June). Building Blocks, (7), 5-6.

Summary of background, purpose and objectives, and scope of negotiations of the new federal claims policy, including extinguishment.

5-58   Fenge, T. (1993, March). Sorting It Out in the Northwest Territories. Northern Perspectives, 21(1), 2-3.

Briefly outlines some of the issues and concerns which must be dealt with in the New Western Territory now that a Nunavut Agreement has been reached.

5-59   Few Concerns But GNWT Favourable to Claims Review Report. (1986, June). Building Blocks, (2), 3.

Discussion of the content of the "Coolican Report" to study comprehensive claims as a basis for a new federal government policy, and of response to it by the Government of the Northwest Territories.

5-60   The First Nations: a Report on the Self-Government Bill. (1984). Ottawa, Ont.: s.n.

Response of the First (Indian) Nations to the proposed Act Relating to Self-Government for Indian Nations (Bill C-52), which followed the government response to the Penner Committee Report on Self-Government.

5-61   Fumoleau, R. (1976). As Long as This Land Shall Last: a History of Treaty 8 and Treaty 11, 1870-1939. Toronto, Ont.: McClelland and Stewart.

Focuses on the areas of the Northwest Territories involved in both of these treaties and on the northern Saskatchewan and Alberta posts of Fond du Lac and Fort Chipewyan in Treaty 8 country.

5-62   Geddes, R. D. (1983). The Pursuit of Aboriginal Rights: The Negotiation of Comprehensive Claims in Canada. Masters Thesis. Carleton University, Dept. of Political Science, Ottawa, Ont.

Examines the legal basis of comprehensive native landclaims and the dual objectives of preservation and integration sought by native groups through settlements of these claims.

5-63   Goose, B., & Haogak, C. (1983). A Report to the WARM Task Force From the COPE Members of the Warm Working Group Detailing Phase One for Developing Details of a Western Arctic Regional Municipality. s.l.: s.n.

Proposed regional government in which the Inuvialuit will be the majority (Western Arctic Regional Municipality, or W.A.R.M.).

5-64   Gwich'in Comprehensive Land Claim Agreement. (1992). Ottawa, Ont.: Canada. Department of Indian Affairs and Northern Development.

Text of the landclaim agreement signed between Canada and the Gwich'in Nation at Fort McPherson, Northwest Territories on April 22, 1992.

5-65   Hawkes, D. C. (1989). Aboriginal Peoples and Constitutional Reform: What Have We Learned? : Phase Three, Final Report. Kingston, Ont.: Queen's University, Institute of Intergovernmental Relations.

A study of aboriginal self-government (for Indian, Inuit, and Metis groups) in Canada and discussion as to why constitutional reform has not been achieved in this area since the Constitution Act (1982) up to the Meech Lake Accord in 1989.

5-66   Hawkes, D. C., & Peters, E. J. (1986). Implementing Aboriginal Self-government: Problems and Prospects. Aboriginal Peoples and Constitutional Reform Workshop Report. Kingston, Ont.: Queen's University, Institute of Intergovernmental Relations.

Report of workshop held at Queen's University in Kingston, Ontario May 27-30, 1986. Examines practical problems in designing mechanisms and making arrangements for implementing aboriginal self-government agreements in Canada. Also identifies important elements to be considered in design of future self-government agreements.

5-67   Hochstein, B. A. (1987). New Rights Or No Rights?: COPE and the Federal Government of Canada. Masters Thesis University of Calgary, Dept. of Political Science, Calgary, Alta.

This study examines the Western Arctic Land Claim (Inuvialuit Final Agreement) of 1984 in order to determine whether aboriginal rights are extinguished and whether the Inuvialuit believe that they have been. It considers the possibility of political action or litigation to resolve the ambiguity of the term, and reconcile it with the 1982 Canadian constitution which entrenches aboriginal rights.

5-68   Indian and Inuit Education. (1990). Information Sheet (Canada. Indian and Northern Affairs Canada), 1990:5. Ottawa, Ont.: Indian and Northern Affairs Canada.

Outlines the mandate for and jurisdiction of education for Indians and Inuit in Canada, including costs and devolution of powers to local administrations.

5-69   Inuvialuit. Inuvik, N.W.T.: Committee for Original Peoples' Entitlement.

News magazine (published 1975-1985) for natives of Mackenzie Delta area, particularly concerning landclaims.

5-70   Inuvialuit Land Administration Rules and Procedures. (1985). Inuvik, N.W.T.: Inuvialuit Implementation Committee.

Rules which outline administrative processes that guide use of Inuvialuit lands in the western Canadian arctic.

5-71   Inuvialuit Land Rights Settlement Agreement in Principle = Reglement de la Revendication Fonciere des Inuvialuit Entente de Principe = Inuvialuit Nunangata San-Naiyaota Sivol-Lek Ilogaagun. (1978). Ottawa: Committee for Original Peoples' Entitlement.

Presents the land rights settlement between the Committee for Original Peoples' Entitlement and the Government of Canada. Areas of agreement include citizens' rights and programs, selection of Inuvialuit lands, land management, wildlife protection, financial compensation.

5-72   Inuvialuit Regional Corporation (1988). Submission to the Legislative Assembly of the Northwest Territories on the Principles of Devolution. Yellowknife, N.W.T.: Inuvialuit Regional Corporation .

Submission by the Inuvialuit (Inuit) Regional Corporation to the Government of the Northwest Territories on the subject of devolution of political powers to local bodies.

5-73   Irving, K., & DeLancey, D. (1987). What Government Does in the Western Northwest Territories. Yellowknife, N.W.T.: Western Constitutional Forum.

This book is intended for use as a reference document and workshop tool in discussions and negotiations leading to the development of a constitution for a new Western Territory. Areas of interest of each level of N.W.T. government, jurisdiction, authority and potential for devolution, are covered.

5-74   Iveson, S., & Brockman, A. (1987). Western Constitutional Forum: Chronology of Events Relevant to the Western Constitutional Forum From October 1982-1987. Yellowknife, N.W.T.: Western Constitutional Forum.

Provides a chronological record of events relevant to the Western Constitutional Forum from October, 1982 to June, 1987.

5-75   The James Bay and Northern Quebec Agreement. (1976). Quebec City, Que.: Editeur Officiel du Quebec.

Agreement between: the Government of Quebec, the Societe d'energie de la Baie James, the Societe de developement de la Baie James, the Commission hydroelectrique de Quebec (Hydro- Quebec) and the Grand Council of the Crees (of Quebec), the Northern Quebec Inuit Association and the Government of Canada.

5-76   Joint Statement by the Honourable Tony Penikett, Government Leader, Government of Yukon and the Honourable Dennis Patterson, Deputy Government Leader, Government of the Northwest Territories on Federal Comprehensive Claims Policy. (1986). Yellowknife, N.W.T.: NWT Legislature.

Tabled Document no. 77-86 tabled on June 25, 1986. Both governments support the new federal comprehensive claims policy based on the Coolican Task Force Report.

5-77   Jull, P. (1987, March). Northern Canada and Northern Peoples: Some Comparative Experiences. IWGIA Document, (58), 131- 141.

Discussion of the experiences of Inuit, Dene, and Metis groups in the Northwest Territories and Quebec, in negotiating with the Federal Government in settlement of landclaims.

5-78   Kakfwi, S. (1991). Community Transfer Initiative. Yellowknife, N.W.T.: Government of the Northwest Territories.

Tabled document no. 5-12(1) tabled on December 10, 1991. Statement by Stephen Kakfwi, Minister of Intergovernmental and Aboriginal Affairs, Northwest Territories, on preparations for devolution of various powers of self-government to communities.

5-79   Kakfwi, S. (1990). GNWT Reorganization on Political and Constitutional Development Issues. Yellowknife, N.W.T.: Government of the Northwest Territories.

Speech by Stephen Kakfwi, Minister for Aboriginal Rights and Constitutional Development. Describes the preparatory steps undertaken by the government of the Northwest Territories for the implementation of land claims and the transfer of power over resource development as intended in the Northern Accord to northerners.

5-80   Kakfwi, S. (1990). Minister's Statement, Community Self-Government. Yellowknife, N.W.T.: Government of the Northwest Territories.

This speech by the Minister of Aboriginal Rights and Constitutional Development, Northwest Territories, outlines the policy of the territorial government on the devolution of responsibility to the communities from the central government, including the recognition of the Tungavik Federation of Nunavut.

5-81   Kakfwi, S. (1984). Partners for the Future: A Selection of Papers Related to Constitutional Development in the Western Northwest Territories. s.l.: Western Constitutional Forum.

Includes: Address to the Standing Committee on Indian Affairs by the Western Constitutional Forum; several ways to interface aboriginal self-government with public government in the western N.W.T.; the relevance of consociation to the western N.W.T.; Inuvialuit self-government in a western territory; municipal government and land within municipal boundaries; language rights for a western territory; official status for languages in Canada; and development of issues.

5-82   Keeping, J. M. (1989). The Inuvialuit Final Agreement. Calgary, Alta.: Canadian Institute of Resources Law. Faculty of Law, the University of Calgary.

Describes terms of agreement in which the Inuvialuit gave up their aboriginal claim to vast areas in the Canadian north in exchange for financial compensation and a variety of other rights. Examines the legal and economic implications for the oil and gas industry in the Inuvialuit settlement region.

5-83   Key Components of a New Federal Policy for Comprehensive Land Claims. (1987, January). Northern Perspectives, 15(1), 16- 17.

The Report of the Task Force to Review Comprehensive Claims Policy, released in March 1986, recommends fundamental changes to current federal policy. These briefing notes outline the key elements that aboriginal peoples feel must be addressed in the new policy.

5-84   Labrador Inuit Association Comprehensive Land Claim. (1989). Information sheet (Canada. Indian and Northern Affairs Canada), 1989:17. Ottawa, Ont.: Indian and Northern Affairs Canada.

Brief account of the landclaim process initiated by the Labrador Inuit Association for the coastline and part of the interior of northern Labrador.

5-85   Land Identification Project. (s.d.). s.n.: s.l.

Draft of workbook for use at workshops at which Dene communities of the Mackenzie Valley Northwest Territories, will identify and select lands necessary to each community, as part of a landclaim settlement.

5-86   MacLachlan, L. J. (1992, March). Comprehensive Aboriginal Claims in the N.W.T. <u>Information North</u>, 18(1), 1-8.

Provides overview of landclaims, of policy of Canadian government towards those claims in the Northwest Territories, current status, and resource management institutions that will be created as direct result of settlement.

5-87   Madill, D. (1981). <u>British Columbia Indian Treaties in Historical Perspective</u>. Ottawa, Ont.: Dept. of Indian Affairs and Northern Development.

Provides historical appreciation of major themes of Indian treaty activity in B.C. Chapter 1 discusses Vancouver Island treaties. Chapter 2 examines Treaty No. 8 portion of B.C.

5-88   Madill, D. (1987). <u>Treaty Research Report, Treaty Eight</u>. Ottawa, Ont.: Treaties and Historical Research Centre. Indian and Northern Affairs Canada.

This account of the negotiation, terms and signing of Treaty 8, which covered Indians in northern Alberta, Northeastern British Columbia, and part of the Northwest Territories, includes the historical background terms and conditions, implications, the text of the treaty, maps, a list of original bands and reserves, and a bibliography.

5-89   Malloch, L. (1984). <u>Dene Government, Past and Future: A Traditional Dene Model of Government and Its Implications For Constitutional Development in the Northwest Territories Today</u>. Yellowknife, N.W.T.: Western Constitutional Forum.

Based on a five-day workshop held in Edzo, N.W.T. in January, 1984. Dene representatives together with staff of the Western Constitutional Forum worked at describing traditional Dene self-government and ways in which it could be adapted to form a new government of the N.W.T.

5-90   Malone, M. (1986). <u>Financing Aboriginal Self-Government in Canada</u>. Aboriginal Peoples and Constitutional Reform. Background Paper, 9. Kingston, Ont.: Queen's University, Institute of Intergovernmental Relations.

Reviews existing financial arrangements facing aboriginal institutions, as well as current practice in financing Canadian governments - federal, provincial, regional and local. Develops criteria with which to analyze options for financing aboriginal self-government. Concludes that block funding is the key, and that constitutional change is required.

5-91   Malone, S. M. (1983). <u>Guaranteed Representation of Aboriginal Peoples in Institutions of Public Government</u>. Yellowknife, N.W.T.: Legislative Assembly Special Committee on Constitutional Development.

Suggests a ranking of main issues to be considered to ensure aboriginal participation in the constitutional development of the N.W.T.

5-92   Marvin Shaffer & Associates (1984). Impact of Division on Distribution of
        NWT Non-Renewable Resource Wealth . Yellowknife, N.W.T.: Western
        Constitutional Forum.

        Provides background information on non-renewable resource wealth in the
        Northwest Territories and the related revenues and employment they may
        generate in order to assist the Alliance of Western and Nunavut
        Constitutional Forums in assessing how these resources and potential
        revenue will be distributed by division.

5-93   May, E. P. (1979). The Nishga Land Claim: 1873-1973. Masters Thesis, Simon
        Fraser University, Dept. of History, Burnaby, B.C.

        Documentation of the lengthy dispute over a title claim to an area of
        approximately 4,600 sq. miles in the Nass River Valley by the Nishga tribe
        of British Columbia. Includes an examination of the concept of what
        constitutes such title both in historical and legal terms.

5-94   McCullum, H. M. (1976). The Dene-Land and Unity for the Native People of
        the Mackenzie Valley: A Statement of Rights. Yellowknife, N.W.T.: Dene
        of the N.W.T.

        Describes the Dene people and their landclaims. Includes the agreement-in-
        principle.

5-95   McInnes, S. (1988, February). The Quebec Referendum Debate: Implications
        For Inuit and Nunavut. ITC News, 13.

        Discussion of possible effects of the referendum on the political future of
        Quebec to be held in the spring of 1980, on negotiations for Nunavut.

5-96   McKnight, B. (1986). Speaking Notes For the Honourable Bill McKnight,
        Minister of Indian Affairs and Northern Development on Comprehensive
        Claims Policy: December 18, 1986. Ottawa, Ont.: Indian and Northern
        Affairs Canada.

        Text of speech to the House of Commons describing the major elements in
        a new federal government policy on comprehensive claims "Living Treaties,
        Lasting Agreements" (Coolican Report).

5-97   McNeil, K. (1982). Native Claims in Rupert's Land and the North-Western
        Territory: Canada's Constitutional Obligations. Studies in Aboriginal
        Rights, 5. Saskatoon, Sask.: University of Saskatchewan, Native Law
        Centre.

        An examination of the nature and extent of the obligation of the Canadian
        government to settle the aboriginal landclaims in Rupert's Land and the
        North-Western Territory from the orders transferring the land in 1870.

5-98   Memorandum of Understanding Regarding Devolution and Constitutional
        Development in the Northwest Territories. (1986). Yellowknife, N.W.T.:
        Government of the N.W.T.

        Draft of understanding between the territorial government and five native
        organizations in the Northwest Territories on the manner and sequence of
        devolution of powers, with the definition of a Nunavut/Denendeh boundary
        being a priority.

5-99   Merritt, J. (1987, January). In Search of Common Ground: Ottawa Rethinks Its
        Approach to Comprehensive Claims. Northern Perspectives, 15(1), 1-4.

        The article offers background to the Coolican report, and an over-all
        summary of the direction of the report.

5-100   Merritt, J. (1984). Background Paper: A Review of Federal Land-Claims
        Policy. In National and Regional Interests in the North: Third National
        Workshop on People, Resources, and the Environment North of 60,
        Yellowknife, N.W.T. 1-3 June 1983, (pp. 71-86). Ottawa, Ont.: Canadian
        Arctic Resources Committee.

        Summary and critique of "In All Fairness", the Federal Government position
        on native landclaims, including a discussion of the consequences of flexible
        response, suggestions for improvement in the negotiating process, and
        changes in federal expectations for native peoples.

5-101   Miller, J. R. (1991). Skyscrapers Hide the Heavens: A History of Indian-White
        Relations in Canada. Toronto, Ont.: University of Toronto Press.

        History of the social, economic, and institutional relationship between
        native Indians and whites in Canada, including cultural assimilation and
        Indian-White political dealings.

5-102   Miller, J. R. (1991). Sweet Promises: A Reader on Indian-White Relations in
        Canada. Toronto, Ont.: University of Toronto Press.

        Companion volume to earlier work: "Skyscrapers Hide the Heavens".
        Relevant articles include civil Indian policy, treaties and reserves, the
        Northwest Rebellion, the emergence of native political organization,
        differing attitudes towards the environment, and the struggle for aboriginal
        rights and contemporary landclaims disputes.

5-103   Morissest, J. (1981, June). The Aboriginal Nationhood, The Northern Challenge
        and the Construction of Canadian Unity. Queen's Quarterly, 237-249.

        Discussion of the "colonial" attitude of central government in Canada
        towards the north and of all levels of government towards aboriginal
        peoples, and of the southern belief that inclusion of the north will create and
        complete Canadian unity.

5-104   Morrison, W. R. (1985). <u>A Survey of the History and Claims of the Native Peoples of Northern Canada</u>. Ottawa, Ont.: Department of Indian Affairs and Northern Development.

Includes chapters on the Yukon, Mackenzie, Nunavut, northern Quebec and Labrador landclaims.

5-105   Morrow, J. (1973). Re Paulette's Application, etc. N.W.T.: Northwest Territories Supreme Court. <u>Western Weekly Reports</u>, (6).

Judgment regarding caveat filed on 400,000 square miles of N.W.T. based on aboriginal rights.

5-106   Morrow, W. G. (1973). <u>Reasons for Judgment in the Matter of an Application by Chief Francois Paulette et al to Lodge a Certain Caveat With the Registrar of Titles of the Land Titles Office for the Northwest Territories (No. 2)</u>. n.l.: s.n.

Reasons for Judgment in the application to restrain development on Dene lands in the Mackenzie Valley.

5-107   Morse, B. W., Rosen, G., & LeClair, M. (1986). <u>A Discussion Paper on Aboriginal Self-Government: Comparisons of the Canadian and International Experience and a Metis Perspective</u>. s.l.: s.n.

This preliminary document is intended to provide the basis for a position paper on Metis self-government in Canada. It includes definitions, constitutional implications, legal aspects and comparisons with Australia and Greenland.

5-108   Morse, B. W. (1989). <u>Aboriginal Peoples and the Law: Indian, Metis and Inuit Rights in Canada</u>. Carleton Library Series, 131. Ottawa, Ont.: Carleton University Press.

Revised edition of 1985 publication, including excerpts of selected materials and original text relating to critical issues in the field of native peoples and the law, including Indian, Inuit and Metis. Focuses primarily on Canadian law and aboriginal and treaty rights, and includes international law and taxation.

5-109   Morse, B. W. (1987). <u>Providing Land Use and Resources for Aboriginal Peoples</u>. Kingston, Ont.: Queen's University, Institute of Intergovernmental Relations.

Paper explores the different means to implement the decision to recognize lands for the exclusive use of native people in Canada, including mechanisms for land acquisition and regimes for holding land title.

5-110   Moss, W. (1990). Aboriginal Land Claims Issues. Background Paper. (Canada. Library of Parliament Research Branch), BP- 237E. Ottawa, Ont.: Library of Parliament, Research Branch.

This paper describes specific claims policy, comprehensive claims policy, and the issues of claims policy such as distinguishing between specific and comprehensive claims, conflicts of interest, extinguishment of aboriginal title, aboriginal title "superseded by law" and exclusion of self-government agreements from landclaims agreements.

5-111   Moss, W. (1991). B.C. Aboriginal Title Case (Delgamuukw v. the Queen). Background paper (Canada. Library of Parliament. Research Branch), BP-258E. Ottawa, Ont.: Law and Government Division, Research Branch, Library of Parliament.

This paper summarizes the issues, proceedings and findings of a significant court case brought by Gitskan and Wet'suwet'en chiefs in British Columbia against the Crown, to determine whether native peoples have sovereignty over the land, as opposed to the government view of aboriginal rights as a right to use and occupy Crown land for subsistence and cultural purposes.

5-112   Munro, J. C. (1984). Response of the Government to the Report of the Special Committee on Indian Self-Government = Reponse du Gouvernement au Rapport du Comite Special sur L'Autonomie Politidque des Indiens. Ottawa, Ont.: Dept. of Indian and Northern Development.

Response of the Canadian federal government to the Special Committee report supporting the concept of self-government (Penner Committee) for native peoples.

5-113   Nisga'a Tribal Council Comprehensive Land Claim. (1990). Information Sheet. (Canada. Indian and Northern Affairs Canada), 1990:31. Ottawa, Ont.: Indian and Northern Affairs Canada.

Summary of the landclaim made by the Nisga'a Indian Band of the Nass Valley in British Columbia.

5-114   The Nishga People of the Naas River in Northwestern British Columbia (1976). Citizens Plus: Nishga Land is Not For Sale. New Aiyansh, B.C.: Nishga Tribal Council.

Statement of the position of the Nishga Tribal Council, British Columbia, on land rights and ownership, and brief history of negotiations with government, including the Calder Case.

5-115   Nishga Tribal Council (1980). Submissions of the Nishga Tribal Council to the Special Joint Committee of the Senate and House of Commons on the Constitution of Canada. s.l.: s.n.

Statement on behalf of the 4,000 Nishga Indians of Northwestern B.C. regarding the patriation of the British North America Act.

5-116   Northeastern Quebec Agreement. (1978). Montreal, Que.: Naskapi
         Development Corp.

         Agreement entered into in 1978 between members of the Naskapi Band of
         Schefferville, government of Quebec and Canada, James Bay Energy
         Corporation, James Bay Development Corporation, Hydro-Quebec, Grand
         Council of the Crees, and Northern Quebec Inuit Association. Provides
         details of Naskapi surrender of claims and rights to land in Quebec in return
         for certain rights and privileges.

5-117   Northwest Territories (1985). Submission of the Government of the Northwest
         Territories to the Comprehensive Claims Policy Review Task Force.
         Yellowknife, N.W.T.: Northwest Territories Canada, Aboriginal Rights and
         Constitutional Development.

         Outline of the position of the Government of the Northwest Territories on
         the scope and form of negotiations on comprehensive landclaims for Dene,
         Metis, and Inuit with an emphasis on an open and flexible approach to
         preserving aboriginal rights.

5-118   Northwest Territories. Aboriginal Rights and Constitutional Development
         Secretariat. (1982). Discussion Paper on the Denendeh Government
         Proposal. Western Arctic Constitutional Conference (2nd). , Yellowknife,
         N.W.T., 1982, September 14 Yellowknife, N.W.T.: The Secretariat.

         This paper considers in detail ten major issues (senate, residency, founding
         principles, councils and assemblies, guaranteed representation, finance,
         resources, land ownership, constitutional amendments, form of government,
         and division of powers) to be discussed at a conference on the proposed
         Denendeh territory (western Northwest Territories).

5-119   Northwest Territories. Aboriginal Rights and Constitutional Development
         Secretariat (1986). Creating a Better Tomorrow: Aboriginal Claims in the
         Northwest Territories. Yellowknife, N.W.T.: Aboriginal Rights and
         Constitutional Development Secretariat.

         Document tabled in N.W.T Legislature Oct. 21, 1986. Background
         information to give an understanding of what landclaims are all about, who
         is involved in the process of negotiating a settlement and how the interests
         of all people are being looked after.

5-120   Northwest Territories. Aboriginal Rights and Constitutional Development
         Secretariat (1986). Government of the Northwest Territories Response to
         the Report of the Task Force to Review Comprehensive Claims "Living
         Treaties: Lasting Agreements". Yellowknife, N.W.T.: Northwest
         Territories. Aboriginal Rights and Constitutional Development Secretariat.

         Tabled document no. 59-86(1) tabled on June 10, 1986. This report
         focuses on key issues that, from the N.W.T. government perspective, must
         be addressed fully in any new comprehensive claims policy that may be
         developed.

5-121   Northwest Territories. Commission for Constitutional Development (1991). How Can We Live Together?" Toward a Common Future in the Western Northwest Territories. Yellowknife, N.W.T.: The Commission.

Public discussion paper on political and constitutional development in the western Northwest Territories (Denendeh) outlining possible forms and directions of government and constitution in the area of the Territories not in Nunavut. Includes outline of existing division of powers, summary history of constitutional change in the North and glossary of terms.

5-122   Northwest Territories. Commission for Constitutional Development (1992). Interim Report. Yellowknife, N.W.T.: The Commission.

Tabled document no. 21-12(2) tabled on March 9, 1992. Report of hearings held in communities of the western Northwest Territories by the Commission for Constitutional Development, concerning the creation of the New Western Territory (Denendeh or Nahendeh) after the formation of Nunavut. Includes commentary on a new constitution, aboriginal and treaty rights, schedule of hearings and terms of reference.

5-123   Northwest Territories. Commission for Constitutional Development (1992). Phase 1 Report: Working Toward a Common Future. Yellowknife, N.W.T.: s.n.

This study originated with the Committee of Political Leaders of the western Northwest Territories who established the Commission for Constitutional Development, which held public hearings on government of the proposed New Western Territory. The report includes proposals for name, geographic area, First people's rights, orders of government, possible districts, institutions and a draft constitution.

5-124   Northwest Territories. Commission for Constitutional Development (1991). Terms of Reference. Yellowknife, N.W.T.: s.n.

Tabled document no. 115-91(1) tabled on July 3, 1991. Terms of reference for the Northwest Territories Commission for Constitutional Development, which aims to develop a comprehensive constitutional proposal for the regions of the Territories remaining after the creation of Nunavut.

5-125   Northwest Territories Executive Council (1991). A Position Paper on Political and Constitutional Development Presented by the Executive Council, Government of the Northwest Territories to the Legislative Assembly. Yellowknife, N.W.T.: Government of the Northwest Territories.

Statement of the views of the Executive Council of the Government of the Northwest Territories on current constitutional issues to be settled before 1997: landclaims, division (Nunavut and a new region), Northern Accord, devolution of land and water regulation, constitutional development, self- government, national issues, and provincial status.

5-126   Northwest Territories Legislative Assembly (1992). <u>Report of the Special
        Committee on Constitutional Reform on the Multilateral Meetings on the
        Constitution and First Ministers Aboriginal Leaders Conferences on the
        Constitution</u>. Yellowknife, N.W.T.: Northwest Territories Legislative
        Assembly.

        Committee report no. 18-12(2) tabled on September 16, 1992. This report
        summarizes the course of various meetings on reform of the Constitution of
        Canada including the Multilateral Meetings on the Constitution (MMCs)
        and the Pearson Accord. Includes the status of the Northwest Territories,
        aboriginal peoples and texts of various proposals for change.

5-127   Northwest Territories. Legislative Assembly. Special Committee on
        Constitutional Development (1982). <u>A Comparison of the Government of
        the Northwest Territories and the Denendeh Government Proposal</u>.
        Yellowknife, N.W.T.: Northwest Territories Information.

        Booklet which compares Denendeh Government proposal put forward by
        Dene Nation and Metis Association of the N.W.T. with current structure of
        Government of the N.W.T.

5-128   Northwest Territories. Legislative Assembly. Special Committee on
        Constitutional Reform (1991). <u>Interim Report on the Activities of the
        Special Committee</u>. Yellowknife, N.W.T.: The Committee.

        Committee report no. 07-12(2) tabled on March 12, 1992. This collection
        of documents covers the reports, presentations and meetings of the
        Northwest Territories Special Committee on Constitutional Reform,
        including the territorial position on the Canadian constitution, aboriginal
        landclaims and the formation of Nunavut.

5-129   Northwest Territories. Legislative Assembly. Special Committee on the Impact
        of Division (1981). <u>Report of the Special Committee on the Impact of
        Division of the Northwest Territories</u>. Yellowknife, N.W.T.: The
        Committee.

        Conclusions relate to four boundary proposals: the Inuit Tapirisat of
        Canada proposal, the Dene Nation proposal, the 1963 federal government
        proposal, and the same proposal excluding the High Arctic Islands as a
        federal preserve.

5-130   Northwest Territories. Minister for Aboriginal Rights and Constitutional
        Development (1981). <u>Discussion Paper on Political and Constitutional
        Development in the Northwest Territories</u>. Yellowknife, N.W.T.: Northwest
        Territories. Minister for Aboriginal Rights and Constitutional Development.

        Presents background information on the Northwest Territories
        Government, and discusses the division of federal/territorial powers.

5-131   Northwest Territories. Project to Review the Operations and Structure of Northern Government (1991). Strength at Two Levels: Report of the Project To Review the Operations and Structure of Northern Government. Yellowknife, N.W.T.: Financial Management Board.

Tabled document no. 03-12(1) tabled on December 9, 1991. This report attempts to provide a blueprint for government organizational and program change over the next ten years in the Northwest Territories, including recommendations relating to devolution of powers to community level, re-thinking of purposes and means of service delivery and an appendix setting out detailed plans and procedures to implement change.

5-132   Nunavut Territory, Canada. (1991). In P. Jull, The Politics of Northern Frontiers: In Australia, Canada and Other "First World" Countries, (pp. 16-20). Australia: North Australia Research Unit Australian National University.

A summary of the political situation in the Northwest Territories, specifically Nunavut, and history of the landclaim negotiations and their significance, as compared to Australia and other countries.

5-133   Offshore Waters and Islands Used by Inuit in Both Nunavut and Quebec. (1988, April). Nunavut, 7(4), 6.

Outline of the Memorandum of Understanding (MOU) between the Tungavik Federation of Nunavut, and Makivik, regarding Offshore Boundaries and Areas of Overlapping Use, dealing with hunting by Inuit of Nunavut and northern Quebec in Hudson Bay, Hudson Strait, James Bay, and Ungava Bay.

5-134   O'Malley, M. (1976). The Past and Future Land: An Account of the Berger Inquiry Into the Mackenzie Valley Pipeline. Toronto, Ont.: Peter Martin Associates Limited.

Discussion of the land and title of the Mackenzie Valley region of the Northwest Territories and the changes that could result from construction of the proposed pipeline.

5-135   Overlap Agreement Between the Dene/Metis and the Tungavik Federation of Nunavut May 9, 1986. (1986). Yellowknife, N.W.T.: Dene/Metis Negotiator and the Tungavik Federation of Nunavut.

Text of the agreement on the boundary between the Dene/Metis and Nunavut claims in the Northwest Territories (to be ratified in Iqaluit, 1987).

5-136   Overlapping Claims in Northwest Territories. (1983). Communique, 1-8325. Ottawa, Ont.: Indian and Northern Affairs Canada.

Announcement of establishment of a dual process to help resolve the overlap of lands claimed by three native groups (Dene, Metis, Inuit) in the Northwest Territories, with the appointment of W. C. Wonders as a fact-finder and R. W. Hornal as facilitator in bringing the groups together.

Claims involved are Committee for Original Peoples' Entitlement (COPE); Dene/Metis in the Mackenzie Valley; and Nunavut (Tungavik Federation of Nunavut).

5-137   Pearson, A. (1984). The Western Constitutional Forum Workbook: a Guide to Laws, Institutions, Powers and Finances. Yellowknife, N.W.T.: Western Constitutional Forum.

Provides information on the structures, powers, jurisdictions and financial arrangements of a variety of governments within Canada in order to assist residents of the western Northwest Territories to participate in developing a government for the new territory, if division occurs.

5-138   Platiel, R. (1983). 14 Groups Asserting Rights to Vast Areas. Musk-Ox, (32), 75-78.

A short summary of native claims by geographic area: Western Arctic, Yukon Territory, Central Eastern Arctic, Northwest Territories, British Columbia, Quebec, and Labrador.

5-139   Posluns, M. (1983). Constitutional Development and the Protection of Aboriginal Rights. s.l.: Legislative Assembly Special Committee on Constitutional Development.

Report examining various methods of protecting aboriginal rights during the establishment of a future territory/province in the western Arctic.

5-140   Press Release. (1987, March). Yellowknife, N.W.T.: Dene Chiefs and Metis Association Board of Directors.

Statement dated March 19, 1987 that the Dene Chiefs and Metis Association Board of Directors approve the division agreement reached by the Nunavut and Western Constitutional Forums in Iqaluit on January 1987, and reject the May 9, 1986 Overlap Agreement on boundaries.

5-141   Press Release, TFN and the Federal Government Agree on Boundary to Separate the Inuit and Dene/Metis Land Claim Settlement Areas. (1991). Ottawa, Ont.: Nunavut Land Claims.

Tabled document no. 137-91(1) tabled on July 5, 1991. Press release by Paul Quassa, President of the Tungavik Federation of Nunavut, on the agreement between TFN and Minister of Indian and Northern Development on the boundary between the Inuit and Dene/Metis landclaim settlement areas in the Northwest Territories. Includes related correspondence on the Thelon Game Sanctuary and Contwoyto Lake region.

5-142   The Principles Regarding Regional Government Which the WCF is Offering to the Inuvialuit. (1986). s.l.: s.n.

Tabled document no. 19-86(2) tabled on October 24, 1986. Outline of basis of regional government proposed by the Western Constitutional Forum to the Inuvialuit of the western Northwest Territories, together with proposal by COPE (Committee for Original Peoples' Entitlement).

5-143 Public Government for the People of the North. (1981). Yellowknife, N.W.T.:
Dene Nation and the Metis Association of the N.W.T.

Discussion paper on aboriginal rights and political and constitutional change
in the north. Proposes the establishment of a new province-like jurisdiction,
to be called Denendeh.

5-144 Pugh, R. D. J. (1982, March). Are Northern Lands Reserved for the Indians?
Canadian Bar Review, 60, 38-80.

Article considers recent decisions, statutes, and agreements pertaining to
the aboriginal rights of northern native peoples in the light of settled law
relating to lands reserved for the Indians.

5-145 Raunet, D. (1984). Without Surrender, Without Consent: a History of Nishga
Land Claims. Vancouver, B.C.: Douglas & McIntyre.

An analysis of the landclaims of the Nishga Indians of northern British
Columbia, beginning with the history of White-Nishga contact and
continuing through to 1984.

5-146 Reshaping Northern Government. (1992). Yellowknife, N.W.T.: Government of
the Northwest Territories.

Tabled document no. 10-12(2) tabled on February 19, 1992. Outline
presented to the Twelfth Legislative Assembly of the Northwest Territories
on goals and methods of reducing costs of government, rationalizing levels
and types of service delivery, and easing the devolution of powers to the
community level.

5-147 Robertson, G. (1988). New Directions North of 60. Yellowknife, N.W.T.:
Government of the Northwest Territories.

This paper discusses possible development of new constitutional and
governmental structures in the Northwest Territories following the
agreement signed in Iqaluit in 1987 between the Western Constitutional
Forum (Indian and Metis groups living in the western part of the Northwest
Territories) and the Nunavut Constitutional Forum (Inuit and others living
in the eastern Arctic).

5-148 Rouleau (Justice) (1992). Order and Reasons of Mr. Justice Rouleau Dismissing
the Claim by the Saskatchewan Indians for an Interim Injunction. Ottawa,
Ont.: Federal Court of Canada, Trial Division.

Copy of the order dismissing the claim of Indian bands of northern
Saskatchewan (Fond Du Lac Band, Black Lake Band, Hatchet Lake Band)
for an injunction to prevent the Tungavik Federation of Nunavut from
proceeding on settlement of boundaries of their landclaim, in areas claimed
both by Indians under treaty rights and traditional use, and Inuit on grounds
of traditional occupation.

5-149   Salisbury, R. F. (1986, September). The Case For Dividing the Northwest
        Territories: A Comment. Canadian Public Policy, 12(3), 513-517.

        "Gurston Dacks's elegant presentation of negative aspects of dividing the
        Northwest Territories calls for a rejoinder, showing why the negative
        aspects are outweighed by the positive ones. My rejoinder summarizes
        briefly the five points made by Dacks, then comments on each in turn." ...
        (Author).

5-150   Scotnicki, C. (1987). Recent Treaties in Land Claims and Self-Government: the
        James Bay Agreement, the Cree-Naskapi Act, the Western Arctic
        (Inuvialuit) Claim Settlement, and the Sechnelt Indian Band Self-
        government Act. Victoria, B.C.: University of Victoria, School of Public
        Administration.

        Series of papers on the respective treaties to serve as a guide to the recent
        history of treaty-making in Canada. Period covered follows the change in
        federal landclaims policy announced in 1973, when the federal government
        indicated willingness to negotiate claims based on aboriginal titles.

5-151   Struzik, E. (1988, March). Meech Lake and the North. Northwest Explorer,
        7(2), 9-14.

        Discussion of the implications of the Meech Lake Accord of 1987 for the
        Northwest Territories, as an impediment to division into Nunavut and
        Denendeh and as a threat to political independence.

5-152   Summary of the Provisions of the Dene/Metis Comprehensive Land Claim
        Agreement-in-Principle. (1989). Information Sheet. (Canada. Indian and
        Northern Affairs Canada), 1989:1. Ottawa, Ont.: Indian and Northern
        Affairs Canada .

        Supplementary information to text of the Agreement-in-Principle, covering
        general and financial matters, renewable resources, land resources,
        administration and land selection process.

5-153   Task Force to Review Comprehensive Claims Policy (1985). Living Treaties:
        Lasting Agreements: Report of the Task Force to Review Comprehensive
        Claims Policy. Ottawa, Ont.: Department of Indian Affairs and Northern
        Development.

        Chairman: Murray Coolican. Traces the background of aboriginal claims
        agreements in Canadian history and law and analyses the new constitutional
        context in which contemporary landclaims policy must be made. Includes
        sections on self-government and northern political development. Known as
        the "Coolican Report".

5-154   Teemotee, J. (1984, July). NCF and WCF Face Many Obstacles to Division.
        Nunavut Newsletter, 3(8), 3-4.

        Summary of the work to be done by the Nunavut Constitutional Forum
        (NCF) and the Western Constitutional Forum (WCF) before division of the
        Northwest Territories can occur.

5-155   Tennant, P. (1990). <u>Aboriginal Peoples and Politics: the Indian Land Question in British Columbia, 1849-1989</u>. Vancouver, B.C.: University of British Columbia Press.

This comprehensive treatment of the Indian land question in British Columbia traces its long history, re-assess the decisions of Governor James Douglas and examines the modern political history of the province's Indian groups.

5-156   <u>Umbrella Final Agreement Between the Government of Canada, The Council for Yukon Indians and the Government of the Yukon</u>. (1992). s.l.: s.n.

Details of the 28 chapters of the Umbrella Final Agreement on landclaims in the Yukon, including ratification, First Nation final agreements, settlement legislation, implementation and self-government.

5-157   <u>Understanding the Yukon Umbrella Final Agreement: A Land Claim Settlement Information Package</u>. (1991). Whitehorse, Yukon: Council for Yukon Indians.

This handbook is a plain language explanation of the Land Claims Agreement for the Yukon First Nations made in 1990 and includes a commentary on each section and list of terms used with a list of boards, councils and committees requiring First Nation members.

5-158   Usher, P. J. (1986). <u>Affidavit: Re Tungavik Federation of Nunavut re Prince Albert Tribal Council</u>. Ottawa, Ont.: Nelligan- Power Law Offices.

Draft text of a consultant's opinion on the evidence of Indian (Denesutine) and Inuit use of areas in the southern Keewatin, Northwest Territories, which was claimed by Inuit as part of Nunavut and disputed by the Indian bands of northern Manitoba and Saskatchewan.

5-159   Usher, P. J. (1990, November). <u>Recent and Current Land Use and Occupancy in the Northwest Territories by Chipewyan Denesutine Bands (Saskatchewan Athabasca Region)</u>. Ottawa, Ont.: P.J. Usher Consulting Services.

This project attempts to document the contemporary use of lands and waters in the Northwest Territories by status Dene persons who are members of the Fond Du Lac, Black Lake, or Hatchet Lake Bands (of Saskatchewan). The areas covered are also designated as part of Nunavut.

5-160   Vontobel, R. (1991, August). Western Boundary Question is Resolved. <u>Nunavut</u>, 10(3), 4.

Announcement of the signing of an agreement between the Tungavik Federation on Nunavut and the Minister of Indian Affairs and Northern Development on the western boundary of Nunavut.

5-161   Wah-Shee, J. (1983). A Design for the Devolution of Additional Powers and
         Responsibilities to Communities: A Public Discussion Paper on Proposed
         Local Government Legislation. Yellowknife, N.W.T.: Government of the
         Northwest Territories.

         Proposal by the Minister for Local Government of the Northwest
         Territories for restructuring local government.

5-162   Western Arctic (Inuvialuit) Claim Implementation Annual Review. Ottawa, Ont.:
         Indian and Northern Affairs Canada.

         This annual review of progress in implementation of the landclaim
         settlement in the western Northwest Territories for the Inuvialuit includes an
         outline of the settlement, budget, description of agencies involved and the
         links between them, and of their activities, and a map.

5-163   Western Arctic Constitutional Conference. (1982). Constitutional Conference
         Minutes: Jan. 19-22, 1982. Western Arctic Constitutional Conference,
         Yellowknife, N.W.T., 1982. Yellowknife, N.W.T.: Northwest Territories
         Legislative Assembly.

         Transcript of discussions by community and association representatives
         from the Northwest Territories on changes proposed for the constitution of
         Canada and the formation of Denendeh (western part of the Territories)
         under a new form of government.

5-164   Western Constitutional Forum (1984). Press Statement, April 3, 1984.
         Yellowknife, N.W.T.: Western Constitutional Forum.

         Press release issued by Western Constitutional Forum whose members
         accompanied Nunavut Constitutional Forum on its tour of western arctic in
         March, 1984. Provides W.C.F. perspective on division of Northwest
         Territories into two jurisdictions.

5-165   Whittington, M. S. (1985). The North. The Collected Research Studies/Royal
         Commission on the Economic Union and Development Prospects for
         Canada, 72. Toronto, Ont.: University of Toronto Press.

         One of a series commissioned as part of the research program of the Royal
         Commission on the Economic Union and Development Prospects for
         Canada. Contains a series of essays on political and economic development
         in the Northwest Territories and Yukon including sovereignty, constitutional
         development, landclaims, and environmental perspectives.

5-166   Whittington, M. S. (1984, June). Territorial Bureaucracy: Trends in Public
         Administration in the Northwest Territories. Canadian Public
         Administration, 27(2), 242-52.

         Discusses four broad sets of characteristics distinct to public administration
         in N.W.T: decentralization, departmentalization, and professionalization.

5-167   Wonders, W. C. (1987). Native Claims and Place Names in Canada's Western
        Arctic. <u>Canadian Journal of Native Studies</u>, 7(1), 111-120.

        The federal government requires agreement by Native groups about areas
        of overlapping land use prior to the settlement of comprehensive landclaims
        in the Northwest Territories. This paper presents research into toponomy
        (place names) which proved useful in documenting Dene/Metis patterns of
        distribution, although Inuvialuit data was less complete.

5-168   Wonders, W. C. (1984). <u>Overlapping Land Use and Occupancy of Dene, Metis,
        Inuvialuit and Inuit in the Northwest Territories</u>. Ottawa, Ont.: Department
        of Indian Affairs and Northern Development.

        Study commissioned by Indian and Northern Affairs Canada in September
        1983 to help resolve overlapping landclaims in the Northwest Territories,
        particularly in the western Arctic area. The report, based on evidence
        documents and information obtained from community meetings, describes
        activities in the overlapping areas.

5-169   Wonders, W. C. (1988). Overlapping Native Land Claims in the Northwest
        Territories. <u>American Review of Canadian Studies</u>, 18(3), 359-368.

        Review and discussion of the areas in the Northwest Territories claimed by
        both Inuit and Dene/Metis groups as part of Denendeh and Nunavut
        respectively.

5-170   <u>The Yukon Indian Land Claim Umbrella Final Agreement</u>. (1991). Whitehorse,
        Yukon: Yukon Executive Council Office, Land Claims Secretariat.

        Summary of the 28 chapters of the Umbrella Final Agreement on landclaims
        in the Yukon, including ratification, First Nation final agreements,
        settlement legislation, implementation and self-government.

SECTION 6: COMPARATIVE STUDIES - OTHER

6-1   Alaska Native Review Commission (1984). <u>Transcript of Proceedings, Village
        Meetings</u>. Anchorage, Alaska: s.n.

        Transcripts of hearings held in rural Alaskan villages regarding the Alaska
        Native Claims Settlement Act of 1971 (62 volumes & index).

6-2   Alaskans Look at Their Claims Settlement. (1984, July). <u>Nunavut Newsletter</u>,
        3(5), 4-8.

        Summary of the public hearings held by the Alaska Native Review
        Commission to gather data and opinion on the experience of native peoples
        in Alaska in the twenty years since the Alaska Native Claims Settlement Act
        (ANCSA) of 1971.

6-3   Crowe, K. J. (1990, November). Claims On The Land. <u>Arctic Circle</u>, 1(3), 14-23.

Summary of the background, character, and process of northern landclaims (Yukon, Nunavut, Denendeh, Northern Quebec, and Labrador) including a map of settlements to date and table summarizing progress and features of agreements, including the Nunavut Agreement in Principle of April 1990. (Continues article by the same author in Arctic Circle 1(4) (January-February, 1991) 31-35).

6-4   Crowe, K. J. (1991, January). Claims On the Land. <u>Arctic Circle</u>, 1(4), 31-35.

Analysis of problems in settling landclaims in northern Canada, including James Bay, COPE, Nunavut, and Denendeh, with comparisons with Alaska and Greenland. (Continued article by the same author in Arctic Circle 1(3) (November-December, 1990) 14- 23).

6-5   Flaherty, M. (1985, May). Australian Visitor Has Advice for Inuit. <u>Nunavut</u>, 4(3), 4.

Comparison of the situation of aboriginal peoples in Australia with that of the Inuit of Nunavut, emphasizing the importance of a land base.

6-6   Flaherty, M. (1985, December). Canadian Inuit Will Meet Alaskan Inupiat. <u>Nunavut</u>, 4(7), 2.

Report of commentary given by Thomas Berger on the Alaska Native Claims Settlement Act and its results, to the Tungavik Federation of Nunavut meeting in Coppermine, October 1985.

6-7   Fleras, A. (1992). <u>The "Nations Within": Aboriginal-State Relations in Canada, the United States, and New Zealand</u>. Toronto, Ont.: Oxford University Press.

This study analyses the roles played by both aboriginal groups and government in entitlements of Indians, Inuit, and Metis in Canada, Indians in the United States, and Maori in New Zealand, including the evolution of government policy and administration, the resurgence of aboriginal consciousness, the importance of traditional structures and values as bases for renewal, and moves towards self-determination, such as Nunavut.

6-8   Foighel, I. (1980). Home Rule in Greenland: A Framework For Local Autonomy. <u>Common Market Law Review</u>, 17, 91-108.

An overview of the 1979 implementation of home rule in Greenland.

6-9   Foighel, I. (1980). Home Rule in Greenland. <u>Meddelelser om Gronland. Man and Society</u>, (1), 1-18.

Background and scope of home rule in Greenland, including the text of the Act of November 29, 1978.

6-10   Frideres, J. S. (1981). Native Settlements and Native Rights: a Comparison of the Alaska Native Settlement, the James Bay Indian/Inuit Settlement, and the Western Canadian Inuit Settlement. Canadian Journal of Native Studies, 1(1), 59-88.

The author describes each of three recent agreements between governments and northern native peoples, the Alaska Native Claims Settlement Act of 1971, the James Bay Settlement, and the COPE Agreement. The agreements are compared in several areas, and against some potential demands from other groups researching land rights in preparation for the negotiation of claims.

6-11   Haller, A. A. (1985, June). Selected Aspects of Greenland Home Rule: Some Considerations For Nunavut. Ottawa, Ont.: Circumpolar and Scientific Affairs Directorate. Department of Indian and Northern Affairs.

This paper examines the institution of Home Rule in Greenland with the object of determining what, if any, aspects can be applied to the structuring of Nunavut with the idea that different solutions may be desirable in Nunavut

6-12   Hansen, J. P. (1978). Home Rule For Greenland. Danish Journal, (3), 3.

Analysis of proposed system of home rule for Greenland by Danish minister for Greenland.

6-13   Home Rule For Greenland. (1979). Polar Record, 19(122), 504-511.

Summary of report submitted by Home Rule Commission and text of Home Rule Act passed on November 29, 1978.

6-14   Jull, P. (1981). Aboriginal Peoples and Political Change in the North Atlantic Area. Journal of Canadian Studies, 16(2), 41-52.

Describes native rights and movements in Canada, Denmark, Greenland and Norway.

6-15   Jull, P. (1992). An Aboriginal Northern Territory: Creating Canada's Nunavut. Darwin, Northern Territory: Australian National University, North Australia Research Unit.

This paper reviews the history and development of the concept of Nunavut, and concludes that its success to date is a valuable example for indigenous peoples in northern Australia and elsewhere.

6-16   Jull, P. (1990). Inuit Concerns and Environmental Assessment. In D. L. VanderZwaag, & C. Lamson (Editors), The Challenge of Arctic Shipping: Science, Environmental Assessment, and Human Values. McGill-Queens's Series in Northern and Native Studies 2, (pp. 139-153). Montreal, Que.: McGill-Queen's University Press.

Discussion of the Inuit and non-northern approach to environmental concerns, including proposed oil development in Lancaster Sound and Inuit rights to the use of ocean areas in the Northwest Territories, including Nunavut, with a comparison to the Alaska North Slope, and Greenland.

6-17   Jull, P. (1993, September). Nunavut Abroad. Northern Perspectives, 21(3), 15-18.

Commentary on the significance of the Nunavut settlement and comparison with claims and settlements in other parts of Canada and in Lapland, Greenland, Alaska, and Australia.

6-18   Jull, P. (1991). Nunavut Territory, Canada. In P. Jull, The Politics of Northern Frontiers: In Australia, Canada and Other "First World" Countries, (pp. 16-20). Australia: North Australia Research Unit Australian National University.

A summary of the political situation in the Northwest Territories, specifically Nunavut, and history of the landclaim negotiations and their significance, as compared to Australia and other countries.

6-19   Jull, P. (1986). Politics, Development and Conservation in the International North. CARC Policy Paper, 2. Ottawa, Ont.: Canadian Arctic Resources Committee.

Author asserts that conservation is the fundamental issue of politics in northern areas. He describes the political questions that arise from conflicts between conservation and development in the proposed Nunavut territory of northern Canada, in Alaska and in northern Norway.

6-20   Jull, P. (1984). Self-government for Northern Peoples: Canada and the Circumpolar Story: A Report to the Government of the Northwest Territories... . Yellowknife, N.W.T.: Aboriginal Rights and Constitutional Development Secretariat.

A report to the Government of the N.W.T. giving a clear and concise overview of the issues in political development for northern peoples around the circumpolar world. Presents some useful insights into the various political developments and initiatives that are of interest and relevance to the N.W.T.

6-21   Larsen, F. B. (1992). The Quiet Life of a Revolution: Greenlandic Home Rule 1979-1992. Etudes Inuit Studies, 16(1-2), 199-226.

Description and analysis of Home Rule, the new system of governance in Greenland implemented in 1979, under which the country is an autonomous region within the Danish Realm.

6-22   Lauritzen, P. (1989). Highlights of an Arctic Revolution: The First 120 Months of Greenlandic Home Rule. Nuuk: Namminersornerullutik Oqartussat.

Illustrated account of the first ten years (1979-1989) of Home Rule, or independence from Denmark in Greenland.

6-23   Lloyd, T. (1979). Greenland Gains Provincial Home Rule. <u>Canadian Geographic</u>, 99(1), 32-37.

Accounts of the events leading to the granting of home rule to Greenland, May, 1979.

6-24   McBeath, G. A., & Morehouse, T. A. (1980). <u>The Dynamics of Alaska Native Self-Government</u>. Lanham, Md.: University Press of America.

Traces the growth and evolution of native self-government in Alaska since the granting of statehood.

6-25   McHugh, P. G. (1982). The Economic Development of Native Land: New Zealand & Canadian Law Compared. <u>Saskatchewan Law Review</u>, 47, 119-151.

This detailed comparison of law relating to land tenure for native peoples in New Zealand and Canada, as it affects potential for economic development of such land, concludes that New Zealand law is somewhat more favorable to the Maori than Canadian law is to the Indians.

6-26   McNabb, S. (1992). Native Claims in Alaska: A Twenty-Year Review. <u>Etudes Inuit Studies</u>, 16(1-2), 85-95.

Discussion of progress and problems in implementation of the Alaska Native Claims Settlement Act of 1971 (ANCSA), in particular the unresolved issues of land conveyances, enrollments of shareholders, subsistence protection, cultural preservation and self-determination.

6-27   Morse, B. W. (1984). <u>Aboriginal Self-Government in Australia and Canada</u>. Kingston, Ont.: Queen's University.

Examines experience of Aboriginals and Torres Strait Islanders of Australia regarding essential attributes of self-government so as to provide information and ideas for consideration by Indian, Metis, and Inuit organizations in Canada.

6-28   Norway's Sami Share Inuit Concerns. (1985, July). <u>Nunavut</u>, 4(5), 4.

Commentary on the situation of the Sami of Norway as compared to Inuit, of Canada.

6-29   TFN Invites Alaskans to AGM. (1986, October). <u>Nunavut</u>, 5(10), 6.

Discussion of cooperation between the Tungavik Federation of Nunavut and native organizations in Alaska dealing with landclaim settlements.

6-30   TFN Visits Alaskan Neighbours. (1985, February). <u>Nunavut</u>, 5(2), 5.

Resolution by the Board of the Tungavik Federation of Nunavut to visit Alaska and discuss with Inupiat the consequences of the Alaska Native Land Claims Settlement Act.

6-31   Tremblay, J. F. (1993). Aboriginal Peoples and Self-Determination: A Few
        Aspects of Government Policy in Four Selected Countries. Studies and
        Research Collection. Quebec: Secretariat aux Affairs Autochtones.

        This history and overview of the policy of central government towards
        native peoples considers the United States (including Alaska and the Navajo
        Nation), Australia (including Northern Territory and South Australia), New
        Zealand (to the Treaty of Waitangi) and Greenland (Home Rule).

SECTION 7: MISCELLANEOUS

7-1   Abel, K., & Friesen, J. (1991). Aboriginal Resource Use in Canada: Historical
        and Legal Aspects. Manitoba Studies in Native History, 6. Winnipeg, Man.:
        University of Manitoba Press.

        This collection of 18 articles focuses on aboriginal rights to the use of
        natural resources in Canada, including wildlife, furs, plants and their
        medicinal and food uses, water rights, general land use and timber. Includes
        case studies from the Yukon and Northwest Territories.

7-2   Abele, F., & Usher, P. J. (1988). A New Economic Development Policy for the
        North?: the Impact of the Canada-U.S. Free Trade Agreement. Ottawa,
        Ont.: Canadian Centre for Policy Alternatives.

        Examines the impact of the Canada-United States free trade agreement on
        economic development in northern Canada. Includes references.

7-3   Canada. Dept. of Indian Affairs and Northern Development (1982). The Lancaster
        Sound Region: 1980-2000: Issues and Options on the Use and
        Management of the Region: Green Paper. Lancaster Sound Regional Study.
        Ottawa, Ont.: Dept. of Indian Affairs and Northern Development.

        Green Paper presenting a series of specific resource use options for
        Lancaster Sound. Also outlines alternative approaches to a regional
        planning mechanism.

7-4   Canada. Indian and Northern Affairs (1991). The Arctic Environmental Strategy:
        an Action Plan. Ottawa, Ont.: Indian and Northern Affairs Canada.

        This summary of the Canadian federal government plan for environmental
        protection in the Northwest Territories and Yukon includes proposed action
        on pollution, integration of the traditional and industrial economics, a
        Northern Information Network, the recognition of Nunavut, and new
        legislation.

7-5   Cassidy, F., & Dale, N. (1988). After Native Claims? The Implications of
        Comprehensive Claims Settlements for Natural Resources in British
        Columbia. Halifax, N.S.: Oolichan Books.

        Study of how a resolution of issues that give rise to and result from,
        comprehensive claims by native peoples might affect the economic, political

and environmental dimensions of natural resource-centered activities (fishery, forestry, and non-renewable resources).

7-6   Framework For a Northern Accord. (1989). Information Sheet (Canada. Indian and Northern Affairs Canada), 1989:21. Ottawa, Ont.: Indian and Northern Affairs Canada.

Outline of the Frontier Energy Policy (Canada), as background to the Northern Political and Economic Policy Framework and the Northern Accord on development of oil and gas resources.

7-7   A Guide to Legislation Affecting Exploration and Mining in the Northwest Territories. (1991). Yellowknife, N.W.T.: Dept. of Energy, Mines and Petroleum Resources, Govt. of the Northwest Territories.

This guide provides summaries of relevant federal and territorial legislation and regulations affecting mining and exploration companies operating in the Northwest Territories. Prepared as an information item only, subject to revision as a result of revised environmental protection legislation, devolution and settlement of native landclaims.

7-8   Holman Says: TFN or COPE? (1984, April). Nunavut Newsletter, 3(2), 5.

Summary of the situation in Holman Island where landclaim proposals by both COPE (Committee for Original Peoples' Entitlement), and TFN (Tungavik Federation of Nunavut), could apply to the Inuvialuit.

7-9   Jones, D., & Robertson, I. (1987, March). Northern Land Use Planning and Parks and Wilderness Protection. Park News, 23(1), 24.

Land use planning in the Northwest Territories is founded upon an agreement signed in July, 1983 by the Federal and Territorial Governments, the Dene Nation, Metis Association and Tungavik Federation of Nunavut (TFN). The article outlines the state of land use planning, the involvement of northerners, the place of national parks, and the need for more flexible thinking in developing a wider spectrum of uses in park areas.

7-10   Lancaster Sound Regional Land Use Planning Commission (1991). The Lancaster Sound Regional Land Use Plan. Yellowknife, N.W.T.: Lancaster Sound Regional Land Use Planning Commission.

Final land use plan for the Lancaster Sound Region of the Northwest Territories including recommendations relating to protected areas for wildlife, marine transportation, oil and gas, tourism, research, defense and sovereignty, and the role of the Nunavut Planning Commission. Includes sources of information and terms of reference for the Lancaster Sound Regional Planning Commission.

7-11   Lancaster Sound Communities Now Have Representatives. (1986, April). Nunavut, 4(4), 3.

   Appointment of coordinator and community representatives for land use planning in the Lancaster Sound region, and chart of the Northern Land Use Planning process.

7-12   Land Use Planning Focus of Meeting in Yellowknife. (1983, May). Nunavut Newsletter, 8.

   Announcement of formation of new working group on land use planning in the N.W.T., including TFN (Tungavik Federation of Nunavut).

7-13   Marvin Shaffer & Associates (1984). Impact of Division on Distribution of NWT Non-Renewable Resource Wealth. Yellowknife, N.W.T.: Western Constitutional Forum.

   Provides background information on non-renewable resource wealth in the Northwest Territories and the related revenues and employment they may generate in order to assist the Alliance of Western and Nunavut Constitutional Forums in assessing how these resources and potential revenue will be distributed by division.

7-14   McKee, G. (1991, July). "When People Talk Together...". Arctic Circle, 2(1), 44-46.

   Description of the role and functions of the northern Land Use Planning Commissions, including Nunavut and Lancaster Sound, and the role of dialogue and consensus.

7-15   Muir, M. A. K. (1991). Impact of Aboriginal Claims Agreements on Environmental Review in the Northwest Territories. Journal of Environmental Law and Practice, 283-316.

   This article examines how three comprehensive aboriginal claims agreements from the Northwest Territories (the Inuvialuit and Dene/Metis Final Agreements, and Nunavut) presently or potentially affect environmental review, with emphasis on their integration with, or modification of, existing and future environmental review processes.

7-16   Northern Energy Accord Talks: Inuit Must be Equal Partners. (1987, June). Nunavut, 6(5), 5.

   Report of progress in reaching a "Northern Energy Accord" on management and revenue-sharing related to mineral, oil and gas development, between the Federal Government of Canada and the Northwest Territories.

7-17   Northern Political and Economic Policy Framework. (1989). Information Sheet (Canada. Indian and Northern Affairs Canada), 1989:23. Ottawa, Ont.: Indian and Northern Affairs Canada.

Outline of the four components of the Northern Political and Economic Policy Framework (Northern Framework) for the activities of the Federal Government in the Northwest Territories and Yukon: devolution, landclaims, economic development and Arctic sovereignty.

7-18   Northwest Territories Dept. of Social Services (1987). Devolution of Programs and Services to Local Authorities. Yellowknife, N.W.T.: Dept. of Social Services .

Tabled document no. 89-87(1) tabled on June 16, 1987. Pamphlet outlining role of the Dept. of Social Services in the N.W.T. and the methods by which Municipal Councils can assume responsibility for programs.

7-19   Northwest Territories. Land Use Planning Commission Northwest Territories Land Use Planning Commission Annual Report. Yellowknife, N.W.T.: The Commission.

Report of the N.W.T. Land Use Planning Commission, the assigned task of which is land use planning through an open and public forum, with assistance from the Lancaster Sound Regional Land Use Planning Commission, other regional planning commissions, Northwest Territories Land Use Planning Office and various native organizations (principally the Dene Nation, the Metis Association of the Northwest Territories, the Committee for Original Peoples' Entitlement (COPE), and the Tungavik Federation of Nunavut (TFN).

7-20   Northwest Territories. Legislative Assembly. Special Committee on the Northern Economy (1989). The SCONE Report, Building Our Economic Future. Yellowknife, N.W.T.: The Assembly.

A survey of the existing economy in the N.W.T. and suggestions for development, including tourism, and for improvements in the economic infrastructure and in social and educational conditions.

7-21   Northwest Territories Government (1986). A Sessional Paper: Political and Constitutional Development in the Northwest Territories. Yellowknife, N.W.T.: Northwest Territories. Legislative Assembly.

Tabled document no. 67-86(1) tabled on June 16, 1986. Outlines the N.W.T. government's political and constitutional objectives, principles, and the current political and constitutional issues which revolve around division, devolution, and settlement of claims.

7-22   Presentation on Behalf of the Legislative Assembly of the Northwest Territories by the Honourable Stephen Kakfwi, Minister of Aboriginal Rights and Constitutional Development and Ted Richard, Member of the Legislative Assembly before the Ontario Legislative Assembly, Select Committee on Constitutional Reform. (1988). Yellowknife, N.W.T.: Government of the Northwest Territories.

Tabled document no. 64-88(10) tabled on February 16, 1988. Presentation giving the N.W.T. government's views on the Meech Lake Accord and proposing eight recommendations for changes.

7-23   Recent developments on National Constitutional Reform. (1992). Yellowknife,
        N.W.T.: Government of the Northwest Territories.

        This speech by the Minister of Intergovernmental and Aboriginal Affairs,
        Northwest Territories, announces the full participation of aboriginal and
        territorial delegates in discussions on the constitution of Canada, following
        publication of the report of the Joint Parliamentary Committee on a
        renewed Canada.

7-24   Reed, M. G. (1990). Environmental Assessment and Aboriginal Claims:
        Implementation of the Inuvialuit Final Agreement. Ottawa, Ont.: Canadian
        Environmental Assessment Research Council.

        This study explores new environmental impact screening procedures as they
        apply in the Northwest Territories. It examines new institutional provisions
        for a joint environmental screening and review process established by a
        the western Arctic.

7-25   Riewe, R. (1992). Southern Perspectives on Native Land Use. In Y. G.
        Lithman, R. Riewe, R. Wiest, & R. Wrigley (Editors), People and Land in
        Northern Manitoba. Anthropology Papers 32. Winnipeg, Man.: University
        of Manitoba.

        This discussion of Inuit and Indian land use in Keewatin and northern
        Manitoba, covers both historical and modern aspects, and the close
        knowledge of the land necessary for native users to sustain the traditional
        economy.

7-26   Robertson, G. (1987, May). Nunavut and the International Arctic. Northern
        Perspectives, 15(2), 9.

        An "Inuit territory" could play a role in Canada's growing interest in the
        international arctic. It might underscore "effective occupation", the surest
        grounds in international law for a claim of sovereignty.

7-27   Rueggeberg, H., & Thompson, A. R. (1984). Resource Management Boundary
        Problems. Yellowknife, N.W.T.: Western Constitutional Forum.

        Provides information on the possible effects division of the N.W.T. may
        have on natural resource management. Resource management concerns
        include traditional aboriginal land use, caribou and other wildlife, water,
        mineral potential, oil and gas and aboriginal landclaim areas.

7-28   Seize the Day: a Report to the Legislative Assembly on Political and
        Constitutional Development in the Northwest Territories, Government of
        the N.W.T., October 27, 1989. (1989). Yellowknife, N.W.T.: Government
        of the Northwest Territories.

        Tabled document no. 18-89(2) tabled on October 27, 1989. This report
        outlines the issues involved in the transfer of power from the Federal
        Government to the Government of the Northwest Territories and in

devolution of responsibility for delivery of services from the Territorial Government to the communities, in the context of Canadian constitutional change.

7-29   Sound Planning Requires Cooperative Approach. (1986, October). <u>Nunavut</u>, 5(10), 11.

Announcement of the formation of the Lancaster Sound Land Use Planning Commission, in accordance with the agreement-in-principle on land use planning for Nunavut signed in July, 1984.

7-30   Swiderski, A. L. (1989). <u>Development Planning in the Eastern Arctic: The Role of Communities in a Comprehensive Development Strategy</u>. Doctoral Dissertation, York University, North York, Ont.

The role of communities in a comprehensive development strategy in the eastern Arctic is examined from a broad perspective, including the emerging processes and implications of the Nunavut proposal and the Inuit landclaim. Evidence from other existing landclaim settlements is presented to provide pragmatic consideration of the potential for change.

7-31   Thompson, R. (1982). <u>Aboriginal Title and Mining Legislation in the Northwest Territories</u>. Studies in Aboriginal Rights, 6. Saskatoon, Sask.: University of Saskatchewan, Native Law Centre.

Study of how aboriginal land title is affected by the granting of mining rights in the Northwest Territories.

7-32   Tungavik Federation of Nunavut. (1987). Land Claims, National Parks, Protected Areas and Renewable Resource Economy. In J. G. Nelson, R. Needham, & L. Norton (Editors), <u>Arctic Heritage: Proceedings of a Symposium August 24-28, 1985 Banff, Alberta, Canada</u>, (pp. 285-297). Ottawa, Ont.: Association of Canadian Universities for Northern Studies.

Outlines the aims of the Nunavut Land Claims Project and the scope of the Inuit claim and involvement in the management of natural resources.

7-33   Tunraluk, A. (1987). Managerial Training in Nunasi Corporation. In W. P. Adams (Editor), <u>Education, Research, Information Systems and the North</u>, (pp. 101-102). Ottawa, Ont.: Association of Canadian Universities for Northern Studies.

This article provides background information about the Nunasi Corporation, the business arm of the Inuit of Nunavut, and describes the "Nunasi Careers Program" that it proposed to Canada Employment and Immigration to meet their target number of Inuit managers.

7-34   Usher, P. J. (1986). The Devolution of Wildlife Management and the Prospects for Wildlife Conservation in the Northwest Territories. CARC Policy Paper, 3. Ottawa, Ont.: Canadian Arctic Resources Committee.

Examines whether the goals of wildlife conservation can be achieved with government authority decentralized and control in the hands of the native harvesters themselves.

7-35   Usher, P. J. (1979). Environmental Conservation, Wildlife Management and Native Rights in Northern Canada. Ottawa, Ont.: Canadian Arctic Resources Committee.

This document discusses the relationship of various uses of wildlife with traditional aboriginal hunting and trapping rights and patterns, and possible effects of changes in government and administration.

7-36   Usher, P. J. (1980). A Northern Perspective on the Informal Economy. Ottawa, Ont.: Vanier Institute of the Family.

Paper prepared for VIF Task Force on the Family/Human Economy. Describes native and industrial economies in northern Canada. Provides some documentation of level of activity in native economy. Reviews analogies and implications for formal and informal economies in southern Canada.

7-37   Usher, P. J., & Beakhust, G. (1973). Land Regulation in the Canadian North. Ottawa, Ont.: Canadian Arctic Resources Committee.

An analysis of the problem of competition for land use in northern development and an evaluation of the function and effect of the present regulations.

7-38   Usher, P. J., & Weihs, F. H. (1989). Towards a Strategy for Supporting the Domestic Economy of the Northwest Territories. Yellowknife, N.W.T.: The Committee.

Report on the domestic economy (transfer payments, sale of commodities such as furs and handicrafts and production of country food and firewood) and its relationship to the wage economy of the Northwest Territories.

7-39   Wah-Shee, J. (1983). A Design for the Devolution of Additional Powers and Responsibilities to Communities: A Public Discussion Paper on Proposed Local Government Legislation. Yellowknife, N.W.T.: Government of the Northwest Territories.

Proposal by the Minister for Local Government of the Northwest Territories for restructuring local government.

7-40   Whittington M. S. (1986). <u>Native Economic Development Corporations:</u>
        <u>Political and Economic Change in Canada's North</u>. CARC Policy Paper, 4.
        Ottawa, Ont.: Canadian Arctic Resources Committee.

        Describes the political and economic context within which native economic
        development corporations operate and presents a model for assessing
        economic development strategies with the range of options available in
        Canada's north.

7-41   Working Group on the Lancaster Sound Regional Study (Canada) (1980). <u>The</u>
        <u>Lancaster Sound Region: 1980-2000: Perspectives and Issues on Resource</u>
        <u>Use</u>. Ottawa, Ont.: Indian Affairs and Northern Development.

        Draft Green Paper intended to stimulate discussion and comment on the
        future use of the Lancaster Sound region in the eastern Canadian Arctic.
        The regional study evolved from the public hearing held in 1978 to examine
        an application for permission to drill an exploratory oil well in Lancaster
        Sound.

7-42   Zlotkin, N. K. (1983). <u>Unfinished Business: Aboriginal Peoples and the 1983</u>
        <u>Constitutional Conference</u>. Institute of Intergovernmental Relations.
        Discussion Paper, 15. Kingston, Ont.: Queen's University.

        Discussion paper providing a detailed guide through the issues facing the
        conference. Explores the legal and juridical precedents in the pre-1982
        constitutional treatment of natives and describes the participation of
        aboriginal groups in the negotiations leading to the Constitution Act, 1982.

AUTHOR INDEX

TITLE INDEX